CREATIV

Best wishes

CREATIVE PEOPLE

HOW TO MANAGE THEM AND MAXIMIZE THEIR CREATIVITY

WINSTON FLETCHER

Hutchinson
Business
Books

Copyright © Winston Fletcher

The right of Winston Fletcher to be identified
as author of this work has been asserted
by him in accordance with the Copyright,
Designs and Patents Act 1988

First published in Great Britain by
Business Books Limited
An imprint of Century Hutchinson Limited
20 Vauxhall Bridge Road, London SW1V 2SA

Century Hutchinson Australia (Pty) Limited
20 Alfred Street, Milsons Point, Sydney
New South Wales 2061, Australia

Century Hutchinson, New Zealand Limited
PO Box 40–086, 32–34 View Road, Glenfield
Auckland 10, New Zealand

Century Hutchinson South Africa (Pty) Limited
PO Box 337, Bergvlei 2012, South Africa

British Library Cataloguing in Publication Data
Fletcher, Winston
 Creative people.
 1. Business firms. Personnel. Creativity. Management
 I. Title
 658.3'14

ISBN: 0–09–174043–6

Printed and bound in Great Britain by
Butler & Tanner Ltd, Frome and London

Contents

■

In memory of Talulah Gosh

'There is an unbridgeable gap between the logic of business management and the laws of the creative world. The art of managing a creative group is to ensure that the conditions are as conducive to good work as they can be, and only then to apply the rules of efficiency. For efficiency is the enemy of originality and it can smother talent, which is of its nature non-conformist . . . this is a lesson which the McKinseys of this world will not learn, and perhaps cannot learn!'

Sir Denis Forman
Chairman, Granada Television (1974–1987)

The MacTaggart Lecture, August 1984.

Introduction

■

What is creativity? Are creative people really different from everyone else? Or do they just pretend to be? How do they manage to conjure up new ideas – for songs, advertisements, stories, designs, fashions, television programmes or whatever – just like that, out of thin air, whenever they have to? Why are they so egotistical, temperamental and undisciplined? What drives them on? Ambition? Money? Fame? Self-fulfilment? How can they be motivated, managed and controlled? How can their creativity be optimized within organizational disciplines and constraints?

This book is about the subtle, sensitive and often stormy relationships between those people who earn their living by selling their creative talents to organizations, and the organizations which employ them. Many of those organizations are vast bureaucracies – companies, industries and sometimes governments – ill-equipped to cope with the wayward ways of creative people, yet dependent on them for the creative products they sell and use.

Today's society consumes creativity voraciously. We watch television and hire videos; buy records and tapes; wear fashions; read magazines, newspapers and books; purchase furnishing and fabric designs; go to the cinema; switch on the radio; send greetings cards; gaze at photographs and buildings and packages on shelves; and are cajoled by advertisements incessantly. Creativity which we have bought, or indirectly paid for, is with us every moment of the day. It permeates almost every aspect of our lives. It is produced in vast quantities, by vast industries, making vast amounts of money.

Creativity is, however, utterly unlike any other product or service we consume. All other goods and services can be, and are, produced to formulae, often manufactured by robots, on production lines. Creativity cannot be mechanically mass-produced. Each and every creative idea comes into existence on a one-off basis, in a human mind. That will never change. Despite the wilder fantasies of science fiction, machines – no matter how sophisticated – will never have ideas. So that industries which depend on creativity will continue to depend, forever, upon creative individuals; and upon managing them successfully.

Managers however, are not patrons of the arts: they are not buying for themselves. They are paying the creative people to produce work which they believe others – usually the general public – will like and want to buy. They are middle men. They must be loyal both to their customers, who pay them, and to the creative people, who produce for them. It is not an easy role to fulfil; and it is not made any easier by the fact that many creative people continuously suspect that the managers are like leeches, living off their talents, creaming off fat salaries for doing precious little.

Less than 30 years ago, the word creativity could not be found in dictionaries. From having had no existence at all, creativity has become one of the most fashionable words, and one of the most fashionable concepts in our society. For some reason which nobody has yet explained, we don't mind eating meat and potatoes, or drinking tea and coffee, again and again, day after day, with little or no variation from year to year. We may eat rather less beef or drink rather more coffee than we did a decade ago, but changes are slow and habits die hard. However, we would not dream of watching exactly the same television programmes, reading exactly the same magazines, watching exactly the same films or even wearing exactly the same fashions, again and again, day after day, year after year. If we enjoy a beer of an evening we expect, indeed demand, that it be consistent and taste the same every night. Imagine watching the same episode of Coronation Street every night. It's almost inconceivable. We may be willing to accept, or even enjoy, a small amount of repetition: we all have favourite records, favourite books, favourite films that we like to revisit from time to time. But even our favourites cannot bear too many encores: variety is intrinsic to the enjoyment of the experience. That is why the creative industries are chained to the treadmill of continuous change. To some extent this is a modern phenomenon. In days of yore, entertainments were so rare they could afford to be repetitive, fashions hardly altered, and people read the Bible so often they knew it by heart from Genesis to Revelations.

Though the phenomenon may be new, it will not be transient. On the contrary, there can be no doubt that it will burgeon and grow more widespread. Professor Desmond Morris, in his book *The Biology of Art* advances the following hypothesis: creative activities are 'actions which, unlike most patterns of animal behaviour, are performed for their own sake rather than to attain some basic biological goal. They are "activities for activities' sake", so to speak. They normally occur in animals which have all their survival problems under control, and have surplus nervous energies which require an outlet.' It could hardly be said that humanity has all its survival problems under control; but in the advanced economies at least, we unarguably have surplus nervous energies which require an outlet. Increasing affluence and increasing leisure will fuel our demands for ever more creativity – both creativity from within ourselves, and creativity supplied by others. The creative industries will flourish.

Inevitably some will flourish more than others. The most successful will be those that are most adept at harnessing the talents of the creative people they employ, to produce the products and services their customers want. Perhaps because most of the creative industries are still comparatively young, astonishingly little has yet been written (or even, to the best of my knowledge, thought) about the problems involved in the management of creative people. This book is the first thorough attempt to rectify that omission. Before writing it, I naturally examined all of the small amount of published material on the subject. Much more importantly however, I canvassed the views of some of the foremost managers of creativity in Britain. This seemed (and I believe has proved) to be the best possible way of discovering the keys to effective creative management. The people who very generously gave up their time to help me in this endeavour are:

Tim Bell – Chairman, Lowe Bell Communications
Christopher Bland – Chairman, London Weekend Television
Michael Grade – Chief Executive, Channel 4 Television
Sir Ralph Halpern – Chairman, The Burton Group
Paul Hamlyn – Chairman, Octopus Publishing Group
Jeremy Isaacs – General Director, Royal Opera House
Wally Olins – Chairman, Wolff Olins
David Puttnam – Chairman, Enigma Productions

Without their insights, wisdom and guidance, I could not have written this book. You will find quotations from all of them scattered liberally throughout the pages, and I should like to take this opportunity to express to them, once again, my unqualified gratitude.

In addition, I have been given particular help and advice by Richard Birtchnell of The Burton Group; Hy Smith of United International Pictures; Victor Ross, ex-Chairman of the Reader's Digest, and Rob Dickens of WEA Records.

Management is not, and never will be, a predictive science like physics; less still is it like engineering. ('Human engineering' is a fatuous phrase, implying a scientific causality that does not and never will exist.) Creative people being what they are, nobody will ever succeed in managing them unerringly. However, some managers are a great deal better at it than others. All management is difficult. The management of creativity raises its own very particular problems. The more profoundly they are understood, the more effectively can they be resolved.

One small but important apology. For simplicity and ease of reading, the book has been written in the male gender. That is, 'he' has been used throughout rather than 'he or she' which, when repeated frequently, is both tedious and awkward. The use of 'he' is not intended to be sexist, and is most definitely not intended to imply that men are in any way better than women at managing creativity. They aren't. If anything, the reverse is likely to be the case, over the next few decades. But unfortunately the English language provides no simple, or fair, solution to the pronoun problem.

1

The Business of Creativity

■

Society today is spellbound by creativity. Great painters, great writers and great musicians become world-famous celebrities and fabulously wealthy. During the twentieth century few human beings' fame can have exceeded that of Picasso, Hemingway or Stravinsky. ('The Beatles are more famous than Jesus Christ', John Lennon once boasted; they certainly made much more money.)

At a more humdrum level, schoolchildren and prison inmates, factory workers and housewives, research scientists and amateur thespians are all encouraged – not to say incited – to express their creativity. Schoolchildren are made to paint, no matter how sloppily, and prison inmates are visited by famous authors who teach them how to write poetry; bonuses are paid to workers who put their ideas into suggestion boxes, and millions of amateur chefs devour cookery books in an endless quest for new culinary delights. Every year, governments and companies devote fortunes to scientific research, while every evening thousands of frustrated executives race from their hot desks to strut and fret their hours upon a stage, expunging the anguish of cash-flow computations and computer cock-ups as they immerse themselves in the angst of Strindberg or Stoppard.

It wasn't always so. The word creativity only began to appear in dictionaries during the 1970s. Its first appearance in the Oxford English Dictionary was in a supplement published in 1972. In days gone by, tradition was valued more highly than change. Indeed in most societies change has been perceived to be threatening. In Judaism, in Islam, and in many isolated primitive communities, patterns of behaviour and rituals continue unvaryingly from year to year, century to century. People continue to live by the Talmud and the Koran; music, fashions and artistic styles remain unchanged for generations. Wisdom, rather than originality, is perceived as the highest virtue. Creativity is either unknown or unwelcomed. To quote Dr Anthony Storr:[1]

'Originality implies being bold enough to go beyond accepted norms . . . Primitive societies find it difficult to allow for individual decisions or varieties of opinion. When the maintenance of group solidarity is a prime consideration, originality may be stifled.'

The high esteem in which creativity is now held in Western society is in some respects rather baffling, since the process of artistic creation is widely believed to be painful, rather than pleasurable. Many more creative people live in penury than strike it rich. Georges Simenon, Inspector Maigret's fabulously successful creator, insists that 'writing is not a profession, but a vocation of unhappiness. I don't think an artist can ever be happy'[2] – a view echoed by innumerable writers, painters and musicians throughout the ages.

Nevertheless, the second half of the twentieth century might be dubbed 'The Age of Creativity'. Or perhaps more accurately, 'The Infancy of Creativity', as it is difficult to imagine how, now that it has gathered such momentum, the development of creativity could ever stop; and those already huge industries which simultaneously depend upon and foster its growth will inevitably expand still further, for as far into the future as anyone can foresee. As was said in the Introduction, Professor Desmond Morris believes this is because modern societies have 'surplus energies which require an outlet'.[3]

Similarly, the highly-respected psychologist Abraham Maslow would contend that it is because many of us have reached the highest levels in mankind's hierarchy of needs; and that our principal motivations are to achieve self-esteem and self-fulfilment.[4]

Whatever the fundamental explanation, the trend seems irreversible. Demand creates supply and necessity is the mother of invention. To meet (and to exacerbate) our insatiable appetite for creativity, the creative industries have mushroomed – some of them old industries which have found new leases of life, others brand new: advertising, architecture, design, fashion, film-making, live and recorded music, packaging, photography, publishing, radio, television, theatre and a host of others.

Each of these industries depends for its existence upon creativity. Not all consider themselves as industries, and not all are happy to be associated with the others. Snobbery and rivalry are rampant in all aspects of creativity, both between the different creative disciplines and between individuals within each discipline. Musicians and architects may not wish to be associated with photographers and advertising people; and individual musicians, architects, photographers and advertising people will all consider themselves vastly superior to other musicians, architects, photographers and advertising people. However, all of them are employed to provide ideas and originality, the raw material for which their customers are willing to pay, and pay handsomely.

The creative industries are now very big business. In Britain each year we spend about £15 million on going to the theatre, roughly the same amount on live music, and £100 million on commercial sponsorship of the arts. We spend about £150 million on going to the movies, £800 million on magazines, £900 million on records and tapes, £1,000 million on sales promotions, £1,100 million on our BBC licences, £1,300 million on books, £1,600 million on newspapers and £6,500 million on advertising. In addition, women spend £6,000 million on outer garments – all of which need to be designed and styled – and a further £1,100 million on their children's outerwear. (British men spend a mere £3,900 million on outer garments, the majority of which, the unkind would insist, have been neither designed nor styled!)

It is estimated that we now spend over £400 million on greetings cards and over £4,000 million a year hiring video films. These figures alone total £28,880 million – nearly ten per cent of the Gross National Product. Add to them the architects' fees, package designers' fees, interior decorators' fees, plus the enormous amounts now being spent on everything from pop promo videos to headed notepaper, and you will have some indication of the gargantuan size to which the business of creativity has already grown. To put the figures in perspective, we spend about £1,000 million on Do-It-Yourself decorating each year, £3,000 million on confectionery, £3,700 million on telephone calls, £9,000 million on beer and £12,500 million on new motor cars. The total figure for the creative industries probably exceeds all these added together.

Nor, despite the stratospheric prices of modern paintings, are we here talking about pure art – though the boundaries between commercial creativity and pure art grow increasingly blurred. For many centuries pure artists, writers and musicians have sold their work, and occasionally achieved considerable wealth ('No man but a blockhead ever wrote, except for money,' claimed Dr Samuel Johnson). But with due respect to Dr Johnson, such creators (including Dr Johnson himself) produced and still produce their work to express themselves and their beliefs, not to feed the commercial needs of mass markets.

Pure artists are independent, and sell their work more or less directly to the public. Commercial creatives* are employed – either permanently or on a freelance basis – by organizations: businesses, industries and governments. A pure artist's work may reach the public via a gallery, a concert hall or a theatre, but its success or failure will depend upon the public's willingness to buy. Pure artists may be guided and influenced by their agents and advisors, but in the end they make their own decisions. For creatives, in contrast, there is always a barrier between themselves and the public: the organization which employs them. And he who pays the piper calls the tune.

The situation is confused because artists and creatives stroll back and forth across the borderline. Weekday creatives are often pure artists at weekends, or at least aspire to be. Advertising copywriters may carry half-finished epic poems in their brief-cases; frustrated fabric designers may dream of spending their days squidging oil onto canvas. On the other hand pure artists often undertake commercial projects, and when they do they suffer the same constraints as full-time creatives – unless they are sufficiently famous and successful to demand complete artistic freedom.

Nor, to add to the unavoidable confusion, is it being suggested that commercial creativity cannot achieve the status of art. Toulouse-Lautrec posters, William Morris fabrics, films and television plays, architecture and gramophone recordings may all be works of art. Modern organizations sometimes succeed, often despite themselves, in spawning great art. But to them the art is a means to an end; to the artist it is the end itself.

* Because there is no equivalent word, and because it is becoming common usage within the creative industries themselves, 'creative' will be used hereafter, as a noun, to mean a person employed by an organization for his creative ability.

Do the creative industries provide products, or services? Some of them make goods – books, magazines, newspapers, fashions, greetings cards, videos; others supply services – particularly entertainment, information and design. It has become common in the creative industries to describe individual projects, even within the service sectors, as 'products'. The managers and executives working on a film, or a television programme, or an advertisement, may refer to it as a 'product'. Creatives generally dislike this usage. They feel it belittles and demeans their work. Creativity is intangible, and ephemeral: how can it be a product? But nor do creatives feel that they are simply providing a service – that, too sounds belittling and demeaning. Nobody would describe Shakespeare's King Lear or Handel's Messiah as a service, nor Van Gogh's Sunflowers as a product, even though it palpably is one. Why, then, should a fashion design, or a radio play, or a pop song, or a television commercial be definable as a product or a service? This uncertainty about the status of creativity pinpoints yet another way in which it differs from other commercial and industrial activities.

Even the concept of a 'creative industry' raises definitional difficulties. All industries and organizations are creative in some measure and to some degree. Organizations which fail to adapt to changing circumstances, which fail to meet and resolve challenges, which fail to adopt new programmes, new plans and new products, soon wither and die. Retailing may not be a creative industry in the same sense that film-making is, but nobody would doubt for a moment that Tesco, Sainsbury and Marks and Spencer are all highly creative enterprises. Most modern management theorists argue that creativity is an intrinsic and essential element in business success. As American management consultant Maurice Zeldman puts the accepted view: 'Creativity for organizations, like vitamins for people, is essential for good health and growth'.[5]

Hence the staff suggestion box, and hence the incentives that many companies now offer to induce their employees to come forward with ideas. The era when employees were required to behave robotically and obey orders mindlessly has long since passed. (Though the reality is that in most companies the fashionable encouragement of creativity generates plenty of heat and dust but doesn't generate many usable proposals.) In any event, the encouragement of original and innovative ideas among people who are themselves not naturally creative is not a subject that we will be covering in any detail, partly because it has already been thoroughly covered in several other standard works,[6] and partly because it is outside the specific territory of this book.

The creative industries differ from others in that the very things they produce and sell are 'creative'. Each 'product' is new, original, different from its predecessors, even if only marginally. 'Perishability is at the very heart of our business,' says Richard Birtchnell, marketing director of The Burton Group.[7] Other industries manufacture and market identical goods, continuously. That is usually what their customers want. Nobody wants every can of Heinz Baked Beans or Pedigree Chum to be different: much the reverse. So while all successful organizations need to be creative, only those in the creative industries earn their keep by marketing creativity.

That is the reason we have not here defined the computer and electronics industries as 'creative' industries: they use their creativity to produce and sell manufactured goods. (Nonetheless it is widely agreed that the scientists, researchers and software programmers working within those innovative industries share many personality traits with their cousins in more obviously creative spheres. Consequently many of the management issues we will be tackling are common to both sectors.)

It is not only those who work in creative industries who find themselves dealing directly with creatives. There can nowadays be few, if any, organizations which do not make use of creatives, at least occasionally. Heinz Baked Beans and Pedigree Chum may be constant as the Northern Star, but their labels needed to be designed, and periodically re-designed. Cars and computers have to be styled; cosmetics and chocolates have to be packaged; even conservative accountants and solicitors now coyly deploy elegant headed notepaper and glossy brochures. Most companies employ advertising agencies, hire interior decorators to do their offices and showrooms, and brief designers to lay-out their annual shareholders' reports. Thus, commercial creativity infiltrates most aspects of business and pervades our daily lives.

The massive markets for commercial creativity generate commensurately massive salaries and profits for those individuals able to provide the creative goodies the public wants. And that's the crunch. Less than astonishingly, the public is only willing to pay for the creativity it likes; and its tastes are far from predictable. If it were otherwise, all the problems of the creative industries would disappear as rapidly as last year's fashions. But it cannot be otherwise. It is in the nature of creative products for the public to like some of them more than others, and to reject some completely. So those industries whose *raison d'être* is the continuous, relentless treadmill of new creative products – new books, new records, new films, new TV programmes, new fabrics, new fashions, new advertisements and the rest – will inevitably produce disasters as well as triumphs. It is because the risks are so great that the rewards of success are so high.

And on the question of rewards, it is worth noting (when a teenage pop-idol's booty or an advertising copywriter's salary seem grotesque to anyone with a sensible, puritan view of life) that the laws of supply and demand operate more freely in the creative industries than almost anywhere else. There are armies of would-be suppliers of talent and, in most cases, an unusually large number of buyers. In the UK, with a couple of exceptions, creatives' trade unions are either weak or non-existent, and the employers rarely manage to fix prices. In every sphere of commercial creativity, from pop-singing to fashion, from script-writing to photography, hosts of creatives are clamouring for work; and as we have seen, there is always a prodigious number of projects available. The spectrum of earnings is almost infinitely wide: from the aspirant novice's pittance to the star performer's gold bullion. The buyers of creativity ceaselessly search for cheaper suppliers. But the competitive market determines the price they must pay.

In the light of the uncertainties and financial risks, it is hardly surprising that businesspeople in the creative industries have for years been searching for reliable rules and principles to help them predict the success or failure of new projects. Beyond establishing the most obvious truisms, their efforts have come to nought. Predictive market research has a role in some of the creative industries, as we'll see in Chapter 10, but it is a small one. The essence of creativity is change. The past may provide rough guidelines for the future, but little more. The success of 'formula' soap operas and publications may, at first sight, appear to contradict this axiom. But even the most formulaic of creative projects demands inventiveness and originality within its 'formula'. (Just as, on a grander scale, great artists and musicians have managed to produce works of amazing originality within highly constricting disciplines.) Formula productions which lack any originality soon flop. Success in the past is no guarantee of success in the future. The public's demand for creativity is unremitting.

Nevertheless, while there are no scientific laws, some individuals are indubitably better than others at predicting the success of new creative work; and some individuals are indubitably better than others at getting successful new creative work produced for them. Such individuals have an eye for creative talent; they know how to get creatives to produce work that customers will want; and they too reap rich rewards. For each of the creative industries is fiercely competitive. There is an abundant choice of radio and television programmes, of films and fashions, of magazines and music, of architects and advertising agencies. In a sense, all of the creative industries are over-supplied, all of them are buyers' markets. So that only the best in their field survive and succeed.

Motivating and leading talented creatives isn't child's play. Those whose job it is to do so never find the going easy – but they recognize it to be the life-blood of their business. To quote Sir Denis Forman's MacTaggart lecture once again:

'For us the people who create the programmes are the most important people in the world, and it is our task to create the right conditions for them.'

Or as Sir Ralph Halpern puts it:

'The creative people must know that they are viewed as an important and essential part of the team.'

As commercial creativity spreads like wild fire through society, the task of managing that creativity is simultaneously growing more important and more complex. The responsibilities of creative managers have likewise begun to spread – beyond their responsibilities to their own organizations, to their shareholders, and to their customers. This fact is increasingly recognized by the leading creative managers themselves. 'The good manager constantly stresses the relationship between creativity and society, the social responsibilities of the creative individual', says David Puttnam. 'The more creative the individual is, the greater that responsibility'.

The best creatives are well aware of this. And it is – in part at least – the impetus behind the innumerable awards which festoon all of the creative industries. While awards are becoming almost absurdly common in all kinds of industries (I recently followed a bus proudly displaying its 'Coach Of The Year Award, Amsterdam 1986') no others are as obsessed with self-glorification as the creative industries. No others dedicate nearly as much time and effort to awarding themselves trophies and patting themselves on the back.

Here are just a few of the glittering prizes currently on offer, in Britain alone: R.I.B.A. Medals, Building of the Year Awards (architecture); Creative Circle Awards, Campaign Press Awards, Golden Break Awards, Rank Cinema Advertising Awards and Television Advertising Awards (advertising); Designers and Art Directors Awards (advertising/design/packaging/photography); British Press Awards (newspapers and magazines); Booker and Whitbread prizes (book publishing); BAFTA Awards (cinema and television); Olivier Awards (theatre); BPI and Ivor Novello Awards (records and music publishing); Sony Awards (radio) – plus a plethora of other regional and sponsored gongs, usually provided by donors hoping for philanthropic publicity. In addition, there is a multitude of international awards, in every creative industry, which Britons frequently enter, and frequently win. Any visiting Martian would deduce that only dogged determination could save the average creative from being pelted by his peers with dozens of decorations as he wends his way from one over-priced awards dinner to the next.

Creative awards are always presented for excellence rather than for commercial success, though they often bring – and are intended to bring – commercial benefits in their train. The prestigious Designers' and Art Directors' Awards, for example, stated as their objective when they were launched in 1962: 'To define and improve the current standards of all forms of Graphic Design in practice in Great Britain'. No mention of 'sales' or 'turnover' or 'profit'. Awards are always concerned with 'standards', 'quality', 'merit' and (whatever words may be used in the citation) 'aesthetics'.

Why are creatives so especially susceptible to such self-flattery? Why do their egos need so many trips? Barristers, probation officers, bus conductors and dustmen all somehow manage to graft their way through life without endlessly ringing each others' necks with garlands. Partly, the answer is inherent in the creative personality, as we shall see in Chapter 3. Partly, it is because the creative businesses are so competitive and so uncertain that any form of public recognition is welcomed, as a means of calming the participants' insecurities. Partly, as has been mentioned, the little statuettes and medals are straightforward generators of publicity and sales. (Though it should be noted that the laurels wouldn't work as a promotional device if the creatives weren't so keen to win them.)

Above all, creatives adore awards because they buttress their importance. In renouncing Mammon and exalting aesthetics, the accolades accentuate the relationship between commercial creativity and pure art. For a few glorious hours during every annual prize-giving the creatives put up two fingers (or anyway pretend to themselves that they're putting up two fingers) to the crude, crass, commercial world in which they work. Watch the faces of the stars when they win. The awards emphasize the idealized quality of creative work, and are a constant reminder to all creatives that their job has (or should have) values that are not merely financial. Managers of creativity denigrate awards at their peril.

Wally Olins, Chairman of Wolff Olins, consciously reminds his creatives of the importance of the work that they do in order to inspire them to stretch themselves: 'I try and explain to them the enormous significance of what they are doing, the enormous power that they have in the world, the fact that what they are doing is going to be seen by everybody, and it is their work. It is their imprint, if you like, on mankind. It may only be a very small imprint, but it is their imprint. I try to make them feel a sense of responsibility for what they are doing.'

That's a bedrock first lesson in the management of creativity.

Footnotes

■

1. Storr, A. (1988) *The School of Genius*, London: Andre Deutsch.
2. The Paris Review Interviews (1958) *Writers at Work*, London: Secker & Warburg.
3. Morris, D. (1962) *The Biology of Art*, London: Methuen.
4. Maslow, H. (1970) *A Theory of Human Motivation*, London: Penguin.
5. Zeldman, M. I. (1980) 'How Management Can Develop and Sustain a Creative Environment', *S.A.M. Advanced Management Journal.*
6. see particularly: de Bono, E. (1982) *Lateral Thinking for Management*, London: Penguin; Osborn, A. F. (1957) *Applied Imagination*, New York: Charles Scribner's Sons; Rawlinson, J. G. (1951) *Creative Thinking and Brainstorming*, New York: John Wiley & Sons.
7. Birtchnell, R. (1989) *Targetting the Female Buyer – A Fashion Retailer's Perspective* (speech on 24 January, 1989).

2

What is Creativity?

■

'Creativity,' says the design historian Stephen Bayley, 'is one of those things that is much easier to detect than to define'. There are of course many such others: love, beauty, honour, truth, wisdom – most, if not all, of the most significant words and concepts we use.

The concept of creation – of making something out of nothing, of bringing things into existence for the first time – has fascinated and perplexed humanity throughout the ages. All societies have their own myths to explain the creation of the world and the creation of mankind. Why? Because the notion that something can, magically as it were, evolve out of nothing is an affront to the rest of our experience, to common sense, to logic. If you want a chair you must start with wood, if you want a car you will need the metal, if you want some milk you must find a cow. But if you want an idea?

For many centuries, indeed until very recently, it was generally accepted that ideas 'just happen', that they float into the mind of their own accord, unpredictably, and that no further explanation is possible, or is worth seeking. The paradigm example taught to every schoolchild is of Archimedes crying 'Eureka' as he discovered, in a flash, how the displacement of water explains the way things float. Less than a couple of thousand years later Sir Isaac Newton was similarly struck, first by a falling apple, and then by the theory of gravity. Neither little story, in fairy-tale form, bothers to mention the vital fact that both men had been brooding on the subject in question long and hard beforehand.

One of the most articulate proponents of the 'Eureka' school of creativity was Mozart. Being an extraordinarily prolific composer of magnificent music, he occasionally tried to analyze how he did it:[1]

'When I feel well and in a good humour, or when I am taking a drive or walking after a good meal, or in the night when I cannot sleep, thoughts crowd into my mind as easily as you could wish. Whence and how do they come? I do not know and I have nothing to do with it. Those which please me, I keep in my head and hum them; at least others have told me that I do so. Once I have my theme, another melody comes, linking itself to the first one, in accordance with the needs of the composition as a whole.'

Then, he continued, the whole work would

'stand almost complete and finished in my mind, so that I can survey it, like a fine picture or a beautiful statue, at a glance.'

Faced with such potent creativity, it is hardly surprising that his jealous rival Salieri suspected that Mozart was in direct creative communion with God.

Few, if any, other composers, artists and writers have enjoyed Mozart's seemingly effortless inspiration. Beethoven was, comparatively speaking, a plodder. He constantly jotted themes and sketches into notebooks, reworking and developing them over many years. Nonetheless, the image of the artist as a uniquely gifted individual to whom inspirations come unbidden, from time to time, like bolts from the blue, is the one that has captured the public imagination. Thomas Edison's famous dictum, that 'genius is one per cent inspiration and 99 per cent perspiration', is widely quoted, but not widely believed. Neither the public nor the creators themselves find Tchaikovsky's following description of the creative process romantically attractive:

'There is no doubt that even the greatest musical geniuses have sometimes worked without inspiration. This guest does not always respond to the first invitation. We must *always* work, and a self-respecting artist must not fold his hands on the pretext that he is not in the mood.'

Before Sigmund Freud, few thinkers attempted to investigate on a scientific basis the nature of creativity. And Freud was far more interested in the creators than in the act of creation (see Chapter 3). He sought to analyze – though his theories have since been widely contested – what it is that drives certain individuals to be creative artists. He broadly assumed, as Stephen Bayley puts it at the beginning of this chapter, that everyone could recognize the creativity of their work.

Few psychologists or psychoanalysts followed Freud into creativity's deep and uncharted waters, and it was not until 1950, in an address at Pennsylvania State College, that the then president of the American Psychological Association, J.P. Guilford, chose creativity as his theme: 'with considerable hesitation, for it represents an area in which psychologists generally, whether they be angels or not, have feared to tread'. Later in his talk, Guilford pointed out how neglected the study of creativity had been. Of approximately 121,000 books and papers listed in *Psychological Abstracts* in the previous 23 years, only 186 seemed to have any bearing on the subject of creativity: less than 0.2 per cent. Some 40 years later the percentage looks decidedly healthier.[2] Nonetheless, in the spectrum of psychologists' interests and pre-occupations, creativity is still on the periphery.

Though the mathematician Henri Poincaré made a stab at it at the beginning of this century, the first determined attempt to provide a realistic theory of creativity must be credited to the great polymath Arthur Koestler, who – being both an accomplished novelist and a scientific scholar – was uniquely qualified to analyze the creative process. His seminal work, *The Act of Creation*,[3] was published less than 30 years ago, and is still the starting point to which anyone investigating the nature of creativity must first turn.

Koestler defined the process of creativity as 'bisociation': putting together two unconnected facts or ideas to form a single idea. (Koestler instinctively rejected the notion that ideas could materialize out of nowhere and nothing. Science teaches that changes occur to existing matter, even if they sometimes occur unpredictably – things do not come into existence miraculously.) Koestler contrasted bisociation with 'association'. Association refers to previously established connections between ideas, while bisociation involves the making of connections where none existed before. According to Koestler, every creative act involves such a bisociative connection, and he justified his theory with many examples from the history of science.

In particular Koestler, building upon the Freudian theory of the subconscious, argued that the creative mind will mull over a problem unconsciously, until perchance it comes across a new and apparently irrelevant piece of information which locks into the problem – even though there is no logical reason for it to do so. The creative mind thus 'bisociates' the new information with the (subconscious) problem and provides a solution:

'I have coined the term "bisociation" in order to make a distinction between the routine skills of thinking on a single "plane", as it were, and the creative act, which, as I shall try to show, always operates on more than one plane. The former may be called single-minded, the latter a double-minded, transitory state of unstable equilibrium where the balance of both emotion and thought is disturbed.'

(It is worth noting that Koestler assumed that creativity inevitably involved instability, and the disturbance of both emotion and thought.)

While Koestler's theory of bisociation works well to explain such great scientific discoveries as Gutenberg and the printing press, Alexander Fleming and penicillin, Archimedes and flotation, and even Isaac Newton and gravity, it seems much less relevant when applied to the world of the arts. 'Bisociation' is no explanation for the inspiration of Mozart's great works – any more than it could be for *Hamlet* or the *Mona Lisa*. The fundamental idea for the composition, the melody, or the plot, might in some way have been the result of bisociation; but the texture and richness of the work is sheer artistry – and the theory of bisociation is altogether too exact and too rational to explain it.

At about the same time that Koestler was developing his theory of bisociation in Britain, a good deal of fundamental research into creativity was being carried out in the United States. Thrown into pandemonium by Russia's lead in the space race, Americans feared that they might be falling behind in scientific creativity. This gave great impetus to a burgeoning of research into the functioning of the brain. Brain specialists had long known that the brain is divided into two halves, left and right. But it was the pioneering work of neurosurgeons Philip Vogel and Joseph Bogen at the California Institute of Technology in the 1960s which established that the two halves operate quite differently, and perhaps even separately, from each other.[4]

Having established that the two halves of the brain are biologically similar, Vogel and Bogen recognized that they can more realistically be thought of as two independent brains working in harmony than as a single brain divided into two, because each half-brain carries out different functions – functions that the other half-brain has no idea how to perform. In general, the left-hand brain handles 'logical' thinking (eg, *mathematics, language, analysis, deductions, logic*), the right-hand brain 'creative' thinking (eg, *imagination, colour, music, rhythm, daydreaming*).

Work by Professor Robert Ornstein at the University of California also found that people who were trained to use one side of their brain more or less exclusively were relatively unable to use the other. It would therefore be feasible to postulate that creative people are those who use the right halves of their brains intensively, while the rest of us coast along using the left halves.[5]

Over recent years a great deal of experimental research has confirmed that the two halves of the brain can and do work independently – even to the point of continuing to function when they have been surgically severed. However, some doubt has been cast upon the neat left/right division of abilities. Researcher Michael Gazzaniga, who was involved in the original investigations into split-brain activity, has carried out what he calls a debunking of 'left-brain right-brain mania'.[6] He claims that:

'Special talents can reside in the right brain or the left. Clearly, what is important is not so much where things are located, but that specific brain systems handle specific tasks.'

In other words, the creative functions are separate from the logical functions, but neither will always be found, in all human beings, to the left or to the right.

Other theorists have developed more specific theories of creativity, all of which reflect, to some degree, Koestler's theory of bisociation and the left versus right brain division. Lateral thinking, the concept of creativity invented by Edward de Bono, relates closely to Professor Ornstein's research. Lateral thinking, de Bono claims, consists of sideways leaps of the imagination (right brain activity), as contrasted with vertical thinking, the continuous progression down a logical chain (left brain activity). De Bono sums up the differences as follows[7]: vertical thinking *chooses, looks for what is right, maintains that one thing must follow directly from another, concentrates on relevance, and moves in the most likely directions; lateral thinking changes, looks for what is different, makes deliberate jumps, welcomes chance intrusions, and explores the least likely.*

In de Bono's words, you can stimulate lateral thinking if you deliberately 'arrange discontinuity'. However, his theories apply principally to the generation of ideas among non-creative people, rather than to the management and control of ideas among highly creative people – as does another well-known theory of creativity, synectics.

In fact synectics is not really a theory of creativity at all, but derives from the 'brainstorming' approach to idea generation first invented by an advertising man, Alex F. Osborn, in the 1930s; and popularized by Osborn and Sidney J. Parnes in the 1950s. Synectics was the brainchild of William J.J. Gordon, who had worked with Osborn but saw flaws in the brainstorming concept. The word *synectics*, from the Greek, means the joining together of different and apparently irrelevant elements. Gordon identified the 'underlying, non-rational, free-associative concepts that flow under the articulated surface of phenomena,' and in a notable description of certain aspects of the nature of creativity, he wrote:[8]

'It is the function of the mind, when presented with a problem, to attempt to make the strange familiar by means of analysis. The human organism is basically conservative and any strange thing is threatening to it. When faced with strangeness, the mind attempts to engorge this strangeness by forcing it into an acceptable pattern or changing its private geometry to make room for the strangeness . . . But basic novelty demands a fresh viewpoint, a new way of looking at the problem. Most problems are not new. The challenge is to view the problem in a new way. This new viewpoint in turn embodies the potential for a new basic solution.'

As this quotation shows, William Gordon, like all the other theorists in the realm of creativity, believes that the mind's 'natural' processes are ordered and logical – and that creativity is, in contrast, a haphazard and illogical leap, which either occurs naturally and inexplicably (Mozart), or when two disconnected notions accidentally come together (Koestler), or by encouraging the use of brain cells which most of us rarely use (de Bono, Gordon and many others).

From the point of view of the management of creativity, the essential conclusion to be drawn from all these analyses of what creativity is, is that despite their differences the theorists unanimously agree on one thing: not only are rationality and creativity entirely different mental processes, they are generally in conflict.

Bisociation is the antithesis of association; lateral thinking is the antithesis of vertical thinking; whether or not they are to be found on the left or the right, creativity and rationality occur in *different* parts of the brain. At times of creation, logic must make itself scarce.

That is not to say that there is no role for logic in creativity: far from it. With the possible exception of Mozart*, all of the theorists, and indeed most great artists, agree that hard, sustained rational thought is required before creation begins. It is implicit in Koestler, de Bono and the rest that creativity does not exist in a vacuum. Creativity blossoms in the fertile soil of rationality. A period of incubation is a pre-requisite, before a new idea can be born. To quote the great rationalist and philosopher Bertrand Russell:[9]

'Having, by a time of very intense concentration, planted the problem in my subconscious, it would germinate underground until, suddenly, the solution emerged with blinding clarity, so that it only remained to write down what had happened as if in a revelation.'

This is an experience which everyone who has ever forced themselves to solve intractable problems – whether in business, science or the arts – will recognize. To some extent it is a technique that can be learned. In youth (speaking for myself at least) one feels it necessary to resolve every problem as it presents itself. Later on, one gains the confidence to know that certain problems can safely be left to simmer on a mental backburner, and that the mind will serve up the solution when it is ready – provided that one has thought hard about the problem at some point, and is not merely procrastinating. Many recent researchers have postulated that the creative process can be divided into three stages: preparation, incubation and illumination. (There is often an intervening, additional period of frustration, which occurs when all the preparation has been done, but the solution still remains elusive.)[10]

Nevertheless, creativity is, in the final analysis, quintessentially irrational. In contrast, business management is – or at least

---

* It should not be thought that Mozart was not a careful and meticulous worker. He seems never to have wasted any of the ideas that came to him, and reworked them into compositions until he found a perfect fit. But he had an astonishing musical memory, and so was able to construct major works in his head.

desperately aims to be – rational. And this means that there is an underlying and unavoidable clash of cultures and processes when managers find themselves in control of creativity.

So a key area of learning for managers is to understand the intrinsic nature of creativity itself. That of course has been the subject of this chapter. The next key area of learning is to understand the personality of those people who are regularly expected to make the irrational mental leaps – while constrained by logic, a demanding timetable (and, usually, a hopelessly inadequate budget!).

Footnotes

■

1. in Ghiselin, B. (ed.) (1952) *The Creative Process*, New York: Mentor Books.
2. Evans, P. and Deehan, G. (1988) *The Keys to Creativity*, London: Grafton Books.
3. Koestler, A. (1964) *The Act of Creation*, London: Hutchinson.
4. Bogen, J. E. (1969) 'The Other Side of the Brain: An Appositional Mind', *Bulletin of the Los Angeles Neurological Society*.
5. Ornstein, R. (1972) *Psychology of Consciousness*, Oxford: W. H. Freeman & Co.
6. Gazzaniga, M. S. (1985) *The Social Brain*: Basic Books.
7. de Bono, E. (1982) *Op. cit.*
8. Gordon, W. J. J. (1961) *Synectics*, New York: Harper & Row. A more recent work on synectics – Prince, G. M. (1970) *The Practice of Creativity*, New York: Macmillan & Co. Inc.
9. Russell, B. (1965) *Portraits from Memory and Other Essays*, London: Allen & Unwin.
10. Weeks, D. J. with Ward, K. (1988) *Eccentrics: The Scientific Investigation*, Stirling: Stirling University Press.

3

The Creative Personality

■

Most of us have, in our mind's eye, an image of the typical artist. He will probably be a synthesis of Vincent Van Gogh, Albert Einstein, Dylan Thomas, Lord Byron, Paul Gauguin and James Joyce.

The qualities represented by this photofit genius include extra-ordinary intelligence, absent-mindedness, commitment, introversion, volatility bordering upon (and often lapsing into) madness, too much liking for the hard stuff – and above all an egocentricity so powerful that it can disregard, not to say despise, the attitudes and opinions of the rest of society. Inevitably some aspects of the pure artist's glamorous image rub off onto his humble cousin, the commercial creative. How far is this justified?

Start any conversation about the true character of artists and you can safely bet an original Rembrandt to a Woolworth's print that within five minutes somebody will mention either Van Gogh, or Gauguin, or both. Why? Why are they mentioned so frequently? Not because they are typical, but because they are atypical. They epitom-ize the way we like our artists to be, the romantic ideal. But not a lot of artists either amputate their ears or dash off to Polynesia; not a lot destroy their lives in blind, passionate pursuit of their art; by comparison at least, most artists live reasonably conventional existences.

Nonetheless, creative people are not quite like the rest of us. It is a difficult area to research, and several studies have proved inconclusive, but there appear to be clear correlations between cre-ativity and personality. Many researchers have tripped over the chicken-and-egg problem – is the artistic personality the result of the creativity, or is the creativity the result of the personality? – but that need not concern us here. An authoritative study by Jacob Getzels and Mihalyi Csikszentmihalyi, at the School of Art Institute of Chicago, which compared art students with the general college population, showed the art students to be more socially aloof, introspective, self-sufficient, radical, experimental and non-conformist – reflecting reasonably accurately the popular stereotype.[1] However, the differences between the art students and the others were not vast. If you draw a spectrum from extreme conformity at one end to extreme non-conformity at the other, creative people will be found in the shades which veer towards non-conformity. A few, like Van Gogh and Gauguin, will be far out on the extreme edge. The great majority will differ from the norm in less obvious ways. This is as true of commercial creatives as it is of pure artists. And it is essential for the creative manager to identify and understand the differences.

To quote Michael Badawy, professor of technical management and applied behavioural sciences at Virginia Polytechnic Institute, Virginia, in his perceptive essay, *How to Prevent Creativity Mismanagement*:[2]

'Many managers do not apply (or even sometimes misapply) what behavioural scientists have learned about creativity and creative environments. This leads to mismanagement and poor results. Managers seem to do more to stifle creativity than to induce it. The most common mistake managers make is to attempt to manage highly creative individuals using the same standards they apply to the more conventional members of the work team.'

Christopher Bland, Chairman of London Weekend Television, expresses it thus:

'They start out differently, and their imperatives are different too. Not that they're all the same. But in terms of what interests them and what drives them, plainly they are different to ordinary people. They don't, in many cases, care about making money, either for the company, or sometimes even for themselves. And that is a distinction between them and the ordinary manager of an iron foundry. He's really in the business of making money. No doubt he wants to make decent castings as well, but it's in that order.'

Tim Bell, Chairman of Lowe Bell Communications, shares this view:

'Their motivations are different, their objectives are different and their attitudes are different. It's a bizarre thought, but the fact that they look different suggests that they are different. They don't like wearing suits, they like looking scruffy, they like to wear whatever the latest fashion is. They don't like offices with desks and filing cabinets and traditional office furniture. They're not commercial, yet they're in highly commercial businesses. They are different in the way they approach life.'

Sigmund Freud believed that these differences could be explained by the fact that the urge to create is caused by frustration, because all creativity involves fantasy and 'a happy person never fantasies, only an unsatisfied one'.[3] He felt creativity to be a substitute for other, more normal activities and therefore deduced that it resulted from neuroses and failure. Today, few if any analysts of creativity accept Freud's thesis in its entirety. Nevertheless, it is widely agreed that creatives are particularly insecure, in their relations both with themselves and with others. While Freud argues that their insecurity is caused by frustration, those who work with creatives offer a simpler explanation. As David Puttnam says:

'Basically creative people are people who are prepared to be judged by their output. That's a tremendously important decision in life: "I did that – do you think I'm worthy?" Creative people have a need to communicate or articulate their thoughts. That's important to them. And many of them have a need to entertain and to be appreciated. These are the differences which separate them out.'

It is difficult to over-estimate the effect that 'being judged by their output' has on the creative personality. For many artists, writes Dr Anthony Storr in The Dynamics of Creation:[4]

'The work, rather than the person, becomes the focus of self-esteem . . . To mind more about one's book or one's painting than one does about oneself will seem strange to those who are sure enough of themselves to be themselves in social relations. But if a book or a painting contains more of the real person than is ever shown in ordinary life, it is not surprising that the producer of it is hyper-sensitive.'

Pure artists and commercial creatives are unique in the way that they are personally associated with their endeavours. (Only politicians and sportspeople are equally subject to the cult of the personality; and often with similar psychological results.) The vast majority of the world's workers, in the vast majority of jobs, do their work anonymously. But every film, television and radio production begins and/or ends with the names of the actors, writer, director, producer and all the subsidiary creative employees; journalists get by-lines; photographers have their identities pressed hard against their pictures; architects and fashion designers become household names. Who can name the chairman of Unilever, or the chief executive of Barclays Bank, let alone the financial director of British Telecom or the production director of Shell?

While the names of the innumerable managers and executives who keep the wheels of industry turning are never seen in lights, the names of creatives glitter throughout the world. Indeed recent legislation[5] gives certain creatives, uniquely, the right to be identified whenever their work is published or is 'issued to the public'; and, also uniquely, gives them the right to object to 'derogatory' treatment of their work. ('Derogatory' here means any treatment which amounts to distortion or mutilation of the work, or is otherwise prejudicial to the honour or reputation of the creative.)

Indubitably creatives crave and enjoy fame. Freud considered it to be one of the essential creative drives. But the reverse side of the coin of fame, is blame. To be personally identified with your work when things go right is delightful: when things go wrong it's dire. So it isn't only the creatives themselves who want to be associated publicly with their work. It also suits those who employ them. Employers are well aware that this puts pressure on the creatives to do their best. Thus the fame in which they bask fuels their insecurity – and this carries profound implications for creative managers.

The fact that they are 'judged by their output' both exacerbates, and makes them dependent upon, egotism. Most authorities who have studied creative people agree that one of their most notable characteristics is independence. Generally they are much more influenced by their own, inner standards than by those of the society or profession to which they belong. In a study of architects in which the subjects were divided into three groups according to their creativity, the most creative group were primarily concerned with meeting a standard of excellence which they discovered within themselves;

the least creative group with conforming to the standards of the architectural profession.[6]

From an organization's point-of-view, independence breeds several unfortunate by-products. Most creatives are career-driven rather than company-oriented. They tend to view gung-ho company loyalty with a suspicion bordering on disdain. Doubtless that is why so many of them are self-employed, and only offer their talents to employers on a freelance, job-by-job basis. 'Goldcollar workers view their talents as an asset, as their own best investment,' claims Robert F. Kelley, senior consultant at SRI International, Menlo Park, California, and author of *The Goldcollar Worker*.[7]

Yet independence, psychologists have shown, is a sign both of strength and weakness. It often shows itself as combative stubborness, a trait common among creatives, though not necessarily unwelcome: 'If creative people believe they are right they must be stubborn about it,' insists Paul Hamlyn, Chairman of Octopus Publishing Group. Tim Bell agrees:

'The creative people who are the most difficult to get good work out of are the ones who want to please you. That's the wrong motivation. They should want to please themselves. That is the absolutely correct motivation. Stubborness is fine. It is unreasonableness that's not. Stubborness and unreasonableness are different things.'

The problem of unreasonableness leads to the frequently questioned relationship between creativity and intelligence. Tim Bell, in effect, would like creatives to show intelligence in their assessment of their own work. But is it necessary to be intelligent in order to be creative, or – as is sometimes suggested – is exactly the opposite true?

In recent years it has become fashionable among psychologists to dissociate intelligence from creativity, to the point where it might be supposed that a high IQ is a bar to originality. And certainly anyone who has attended university will have met many academics who have immense intelligence but no originality at all. In fact, research shows no direct correlation between creativity and IQ, and IQ scores can never be used to predict creativity. However, almost all highly creative people have an IQ somewhat above average, often around 120. They are bright, but not outstandingly so. Professor

Frank Barron summarizes the situation:[8]

'For certain intrinsically creative activities a specifiable minimum IQ is probably necessary, to engage in the activity at
all, but beyond that minimum, which is often surprisingly low,
creativity has little correlation with scores on IQ tests.'

Once again we see the seeds of dissension between creativity and
management. Managers are usually (though admittedly not always!)
chosen for their intelligence, have an academic education, and have
been trained to respect and respond to intellectual abilities. Lacking
these particular abilities, the creatives fall back upon stubborness,
and appear intransigent because they lack analytical debating skills.

The difficulties might be less pronounced if creatives were better
at editing their own work. Almost by definition, because they bubble
with ideas, the ability to sort the wheat from the chaff is one of the
hallmarks of a great creator. Indeed, one of the main things that sets
really creative people apart is their ability to judge their own ideas.
The role of the artist as editor is two-fold. Not only must artists reject
their dud ideas ruthlessly, they must also be able to identify imperfect
ideas and be willing to work upon them with infinite diligence, for
as long as it takes to get them right. Here, for example, is Robert
Weisberg's description of Pablo Picasso's approach to the painting of
his great mural, *Guernica*.[9]

'Several possibilities for the general composition of the mural
were considered before Picasso began to paint, and the composition underwent further changes while he painted. Likewise,
specific aspects of the characters were considered again and
again in preliminary work and then modified still further as the
painting progressed . . . Picasso is very hard to satisfy and always
ready to try once more to get some small detail a little better.'

The same meticulous process is documented and portrayed in every
author's or composer's notebook, every artist's sketchbook, in the
drafting and re-drafting to which most of the world's greatest masterpieces have been subjected before they reach the public. Such 'editing' reflects the commitment to perfection which is another fundamental aspect of the creative personality. However, perfectionism
takes time, and costs money. So an undisciplined dedication to its
achievement inevitably brings creatives into conflict with management, one of whose most important job functions is the control of

costs and time schedules. The paradox is that managers accept (and even admire) creatives' perfectionism. They recognize that perfectionism is an inherent and essential part of creativity; but they are rarely able to provide the resources necessary for perfection to be attained.

To achieve perfection, or to get as close to it as they can, most creatives put their heart and soul into their work. This aspect of the creative personality is one that conflicts with the conventional image of the artist as someone who lazes about nonchalantly, daydreaming, chatting, drinking, and having ideas from time to time, usually in the bath. That image could hardly be less accurate. Biographical information and psychological studies of creative people consistently show that the great majority are driven by the need to work. And the degree of their commitment to their work appears to be another important difference between creative and non-creative people. A simplistic explanation would be that creative people enjoy their work more than others – and for some of them, on some occasions, this is true. But as we saw in the previous chapter, creative people often need to force themselves to work. All that can be said with certainty is that they prefer creating, difficult and painful though it often is, to doing anything else.

They are not necessarily, however, good at timekeeping (and this may in part explain why others tend to view them as idle). 'Research shows that morning, noon and night are all the same to creative people; they don't work by the clock. Time has a personal, not a social meaning,' as Professor Michael Badawy writes.[10] Psychologist Abraham Maslow observes:[11]

> 'The creative person, in the inspirational phase of the creative furor, loses his past and his future and lives only in the moment. He is all there, totally immersed, fascinated and absorbed in the present, in the current situation, in the here-now, with the matter in hand . . . This ability to become 'lost in the present' seems to be a *sine qua non* for creativeness of any kind.'

This apparently cavalier attitude to timekeeping may be a symptom of a more fundamental trait in the creative personality: the rejection of authority. Since new ideas can only be brought into existence by those who question existing ones, it is hardly surprising that a spirit of rebelliousness should be endemic among creatives. Freud, perhaps predictably, suggests that this rebelliousness against the past is an expression of artists' hostility to their parents – a hostility which, he believes, engenders artistic creation. However, rebelliousness of itself is obviously no guarantee of creativity. To quote Stephen Bayley:[12]

> 'Creative people need to have a sort of vision and a strong moral commitment to changing things for the better. They have to be unafraid of breaking rules, although it's axiomatic they have to know the rules in the first place. So they have to be disciplined people.'

Creatives' innate rebelliousness inevitably leads them to dislike taking orders. Since most business executives are in the habit of giving orders, however mildly stated, this is yet another aspect of the creative personality with which they find it difficult to cope.

Moreover, although the great majority of creatives are not, as we have seen, uncontrollably wild, in every creative industry there will invariably be found a handful who are. And sometimes (by no means always) these are the people with the greatest talent. It may well be (but how could it be proved?) that just as many bank clerks and garage mechanics would be equally uncontrollable and wild, were they ever allowed to be. Lacking unique creative talent, they either restrain themselves or end up locked-up. Because outstanding creative ability is so rare, the creative manager who finds and employs talented people must learn to live with their whims and tantrums. As Christopher Bland says:

> 'It may be difficult, but does that mean you won't work with Callas? How likeable was Callas? By all accounts, not at all. The word *prima donna* comes from opera! To say you can only work with those you personally like – no, it would be impossible.'

Paul Hamlyn agrees:

> 'Creative people are certainly more difficult, sometimes difficult in unpleasant ways. Some of the big, best-selling authors are pretty obnoxious. As people. But you put up with them.'

Michael Grade agrees, too:

> 'If they've got talent I don't have to like them. I have to like their talent. I've worked with a lot of creative people I couldn't stand. They wouldn't know I couldn't stand them. They never know that.'

And so does Tim Bell:

'It can be fantastically frustrating working with creatives. They're petulant and difficult and refuse to pay attention and have different priorities. Dumb insolence is a classic characteristic of creative people and they are very dismissive of everybody else. The answer, then, is not to deal with them but to deal with their work. Liking them needn't come into it.'

Nor does Christopher Bland find anything particularly untoward in this situation:

'Yes, you have got to be able and willing to work with outstanding talents you dislike. Otherwise you'd cut yourself off from a great deal of talent. If you only published authors you liked, and wanted to have dinner with, and go on holiday with, you'd have a very short list indeed. Why should great artists be likeable? Most of them are anything but, and to expect it I think is odd. Plainly it's a great bonus if they are.'

We have seen then that creatives tend to be insecure, egotistical, stubborn, rebellious, poor time-keeping perfectionists who seek fame and are not necessarily all that intelligent. However, these diverse and sometimes complex personality traits do not, even when added together, mean that creatives are nutcases, with bats in the belfry and screws loose. Those creatives who are, in some degree, mentally unbalanced, are a minuscule minority. Naturally, as with Van Gogh and Gauguin, they are the ones about whom well-worn and probably apocryphal anecdotes are often told in pubs. But every scrap of available evidence shows that creativity and mental instability rarely go hand-in-hand. Indeed, the fact has been well-established since 1904 when Havelock Ellis (better known for his *Studies in the Psychology of Sex*) published a book called *A Study of British Genius*. From the *Dictionary of National Biography*, Ellis culled the names of 1,030 'geniuses' among whom he could discover only 44 (4.2 per cent) who were demonstrably insane. He wrote, with evident regret: 'The association between genius and insanity is not, I believe, without significance, but in view of the fact that its occurrence is only demonstrable in less than five per cent of cases, we must put out of court any theory of genius being a form of insanity.'

Ellis's figures, as Dr Anthony Storr points out in *The Dynamics of Creation*, are remarkably low since they include senile disorders;

and the lack of any association between madness and creativity is emphasized by the fact that nowadays one in 15 of the British population (6.7 per cent) is resident in a mental hospital at some point in their lives. Dr Storr concludes: 'For creative work, access to the inner realm of the psyche is essential. But so is a strong, functioning ego, capable of judgment, inhibition of immediate impulse, persistence and control.'

The same important point is made by Dr Jonathan Miller in *The Keys to Creativity*:[13]

'There are artists who happen to have been depressed, frenzied or manic, and who also happen to be geniuses. But their genius does not flow from their disorder. It's something they manage to live with and to produce with. The idea that you have to be in some way disordered to produce, or that it's an advisable state of mind, is nonsense.'

And referring to creatives in business, Professor Carl Hakmiller, of the University of Connecticut, concurs:[14]

'The myth of weirdos running around wearing plaid shirts and no socks just isn't true.'

It has been important to labour the fact that, no matter how difficult they may sometimes be, creatives are not a crazy, incomprehensible species, because it is a cliché that much appeals to some creatives and to some managers. To the creatives it is an excuse (indeed an encouragement) for capricious, selfish, histrionic behaviour; to the managers it explains why creatives are impossible to control, and provides a heaven-sent reason for being unable to deal with them.

To manage creatives successfully you must obviously understand their personality traits and idiosyncracies. But it is equally important – if not more important – never to treat them as oddballs. Michael Grade, Chief Executive of Channel 4 Television, gives this advice:

'When you're dealing with creative people's egocentricity or temperament you've got to ask yourself, "Why are they like that?" And the answer is that they are in a very exposed position. They are therefore very insecure. If you understand their insecurities then you can deal with them. People aren't egocentric or temperamental for no reason, it's rarely a character flaw. We are all insecure in some ways, and our insecurities manifest themselves differently. Some of us are temperamental, some of us are depressive, some are bad at paperwork. And in each case you have to understand why. You have to understand what the job is you want the creatives to do, and find a way to get the best out of them. It's the same with any job.'

Or, as David Puttnam tersely puts it:

'I don't tend to make concessions for creative people.'

Sympathetic understanding, yes; concessions, no. That is another vital principle underlying the management of creativity.

Footnotes

■

1. Getzels, J. and Csikszentmihalyi, M. (1976) *The Creative Vision: A Longitudinal Study of Problem Finding in Art*, New York: John Wiley & Sons.
2. Badawy, M. (1986) 'How to Prevent Creativity Mismanagement', *Research Management*: The Industrial Research Institute Inc.
3. Freud, S. (1959) *Creative Writers and Day-Dreaming*, London: The Hogarth Press.
4. Storr, A. (1972) *The Dynamics of Creation*, London: Secker & Warburg.
5. The Copyright, Design and Patents Act 1988, Sections 77 and 80.
6. Storr, A. (1972) *Op. cit.*
7. in Goldstein, M. L. (1985) 'Managing the Goldcollar Worker', *Industry Week*.
   ('Goldcollar' workers is the latest American jargon term for employees whose jobs require a high degree of creativity, and who are employed on projects which significantly affect their company's future.)
8. Barron, F. (1969) *Creative Person and Creative Process*, London: Holt, Rinehart & Winston.
9. Weisberg, R. W. (1986) *Creativity: Genius and Other Myths*, New York: W. H. Freeman & Co.
10. Badawy, M. K. (1986) *Op. cit.*
11. Maslow, A. (1973) *The Farther Reaches of Human Nature*, London: Harmondsworth.
12. in Evans, P. and Deehan, G. (1988) *Op. cit.*
13. *Ibid.*
14. in Goldstein, M. L. (1985) *Op. cit.*

4

The Diversity of Creativity

■

So far, we have implicitly taken for granted that creativity is a single, identifiable thing. It isn't. Little research has yet been undertaken into defining the different types of creativity – but then, as we have seen, little research has been undertaken into the nature of creativity at all. The wider problems have proved so daunting that researchers have been unwilling to complicate matters still further by attempting to sub-divide a concept that is itself as impenetrable as a Schoenberg symphony. On the contrary, most theorists have sought to simplify matters by claiming (or at least implying) that creativity is a unique, quantifiable entity – like gravity or DNA – which will one day be identified and understood.

This reflects neither common sense nor the experience of those who have worked with creative people. Just as there are many types of creative personality, there are many types of creativity; and the manager must handle them in different ways.

In the first place, there are obvious *qualitative* differences. At the lowest level of definition, it is possible to argue that every single act that every single person in the world ever performs is creative: no other person has ever before done that particular thing at that particular time in that particular place in that particular way. ('Can I have the same again?' asks the customer in the old pub joke. 'Most certainly not,' replies the witty barman, 'you can never have the same again, you can only have something similar'.)

A less rigorous, and more common version of this argument is that 'Everyone is creative really, in their own way'. Indeed even chimpanzees are creative, in their own way. Faced with the problem of retrieving a banana from a high shelf, a chimpanzee will build an ingenious (for a chimpanzee) assemblage of chairs, tables and sticks adequate to the task. So – ignoring chimpanzees – you can certainly define all human beings and all human acts as creative; but in that case you will need to find a new word to differentiate driving a bus from composing the Pastoral Symphony.

That is a *reductio ad absurdum* of the argument that everybody and every act is creative in its own way. Obviously there are qualitative differences between various levels of creativity. We can all recognize the extremes, and in between the extremes there is an almost infinitely long continuum. Scattered along the continuum (some of them closer to driving a bus, some of them closer to composing the Pastoral) are to be found cooking cabbage and *nouvelle cuisine*, building a garden shed and building Chartres cathedral, writing memos and writing Crime and Punishment, yodelling in the bath and composing Carmen, doodling patterns and painting The Haywain – all of which might be thought by their progenitors and practitioners to be creative.

Focusing more sharply on commercial creativity, also along the continuum you will find the novels of Barbara Cartland and F. Scott Fitzgerald, blocks of dreary council flats and the Musée George Pompidou in Paris, pub rock groups and The Beatles, 'B' movies and Citizen Kane, lavatory cleanser commercials and the Heineken 'refreshes the parts other beers cannot reach' advertisements, Evans Outsize frocks and Kenzo fashions. Once again all of them would probably be claimed, by their creators, to be creative.

It is no part of the function of this book to get embroiled in aesthetic value judgments (though in any discussion of creativity they are virtually impossible to avoid). But it is vital for the creative manager to recognize and to determine the quality – to use an unavoidable value judgment word – of the creativity in which he is involved. In creativity, as everywhere else, you generally get what you pay for: the higher the quality, the higher the price. As we have seen, the markets for creativity are uncommonly free and competitive; prices adjust to supply and demand with great rapidity. Creative quality, even if indefinable, is always in short supply and in great demand. So that one of the principle functions of the creative manager is to decide upon the level of quality necessary, and justifiable, and affordable, for any particular job. This is an essential aspect of cost control, to which we'll return in Chapter 8.

The manager's difficulties in this area are compounded by the fact that the quality of creative peoples' work is notoriously inconsistent. This is as true of great artists as it is of commonplace creatives. Picasso's paintings and Shakespeare's sonnets are of variable quality, to put it generously, and even Leonardo da Vinci – rightly celebrated for a lifetime of astonishing creative achievement – had loads of daft ideas, including one for a machine which flew by flapping its wings, on which he worked enthusiastically for years. Nor is it merely the little ideas that great men frequently get wrong. Sir Isaac Newton spent a quarter of a century studying alchemy, and wrote thousands of more or less worthless pages on the subject; while his intellectual heir, Albert Einstein, rejected Max Planck's discovery of quantum mechanics saying, 'An inner voice tells me it is not the real thing'.[1]

This inconsistency in creative people's output and judgment is one of the most intractable problems which managers face. It is hard to think of any other group whose work varies so greatly or so unpredictably. Nobody doubts that on average (if such an average could ever be calculated) the most talented creative people produce high quality work more consistently than the least talented. That is the assumption upon which all creative fees and prices are based, and it is essential to the orderly working of the marketplace: 'He did a marvellous job last time, so the likelihood is he'll do a marvellous job next time'. It is a sound rule-of-thumb, but it must be applied with caution. Outstanding creative people can and do charge more for their services because nine times out of ten they can be relied upon to produce outstanding work. Or might it be only six times out of ten? Time and again the most highly-talented and conscientious creatives blunder, boob and botch things up; and just occasionally, to balance the equation, individuals of mediocre talent produce gems of immense worth.

The creative manager must forever be alert to such mutations. No creative industry suffers more from creatives' vagaries than the film industry. Steven Bach, in his marvellous case history of calamitous creative management, *Final Cut*,[2] records how almost every great Hollywood talent – from Griffith to Gable, from Chaplin to Coppola, from Welles to Wilder – has on occasion (and usually on many occasions) produced box office flops. In every creative industry, but especially in the movies, the difficulties of inconsistency are further aggravated by creatives' egotism. And the bigger they are, the harder they fall.

There will never be a watertight solution to the problem, but that does not provide the creative manager with a watertight excuse for ignoring it. It is one of many reasons, as we shall see in the following chapter, why the effective creative manager must never be intimidated by, or in awe of, the creatives with whom he is working.

Another area of creative diversity – equally difficult to pinpoint precisely – is style. In the pure arts, creators of similar stature may be differentiated from each other in a host of ways: classic versus romantic, traditionalist versus radical, spiritual versus materialistic, and so on. These are not differences of quality, but of attitude, vision and style. Such differences are just as important, and may be more so, in the world of commercial creativity. To the creative manager, they are a minefield. All good creatives have their own style; so do most creative businesses. When the two are mis-matched havoc ensues – aggravated by the fact that it often takes a fair while for the problem to be identified, as differences in style are frequently far from obvious.

Few creative people are even aware of their own style. To them their style comes naturally and seems the right way, possibly the only way, to do things. Hence they are often unaware of its limitations. So they seek jobs which they cannot do, or anyway cannot do well. Square pegs will have no idea that they are trying to force themselves into round holes: as likely as not they will be fascinated by the challenge. The effective manager will assess the varying styles of the creatives with whom he is involved, and also know how far their styles can be stretched. Occasionally, perhaps on a small or unimportant job, he will take a calculated risk, and encourage a creative to try his hand at something that may be outside his range. Most of the time, however, it is the manager's job to pick the right style of horse for the right style of course, based on the track record and proven abilities. There are more than enough risks in the management of creativity, without taking on unnecessary ones.

From questions of quality and style, let us turn to another important area where kinds of creativity vary: the differences between idea and execution. Most theories of creativity concentrate on ideas. Almost all of the discussion of 'What is Creativity?' in Chapter 2, for example, was primarily concerned with the birth of ideas. Yet artistic creativity is rarely dependent on 'ideas'. Ideas are, at most, only a part of the creativity. It is not principally for their ideas that we admire Dostoyevsky's novels, or Verdi's operas, or Turner's paintings. The notion of an idea, as we saw, is of something that comes into the mind from nowhere, all of a sudden. That process may well explain and describe scientific inventions and discoveries, but it can hardly explain or describe the writing of a novel, or of an opera, or the making of a painting or sculpture. It hardly makes sense to describe the scribbling of tens of thousands of words, or the dabbing of hundreds of thousands of spots of paint onto a canvas, as a vast series of tiny ideas. The idea and the execution of the idea are patently different forms of creativity. It is a difference with profound implications for creative businesses.

Professor Robert Weisberg[3] attempts to dissolve the dichotomy between ideas and execution by defining creativity as 'incremental' in nature. Because a great many artists develop and change their masterpieces as they progress, he concludes that the process comprises a series of discrete steps: a flight of separate, individual ideas. Perhaps it will one day be discovered that he is right, and that is indeed the way works of art are created. But it seems unlikely. Once the initial idea has occurred the process is much less disjointed, much more continuous than Weisberg (and most other theorists) claim. Of course artists pause, or even down tools, from time to time, to consider and reconsider their progress; but in between pauses they work rapidly, ceaselessly, without stopping to think.

From the point of view of commercial creativity, the significance of this issue lies in the fact that some creatives are far better at having ideas, others far better at carrying them out. In every creative industry there are borderlines, between the origination of ideas and their execution. Both can be equally creative (or uncreative, for that matter). The magazine editor is not necessarily more, or less, creative than the feature writer; the advertising art director is not necessarily more, or less, creative than the photographer he uses. Note that we are not here considering the differences between creator and interpreter – that is, between composer and musician, or between author and actor. Both editor and feature writer are creators. Nor should it be thought, though it often is, that having ideas is creatively superior to executing them. Shakespeare was no great inventor of plots, and rarely bothered trying to be. As has previously been said, few great artists are renowned principally for their inventiveness.

Because they fail to recognize the equal importance of both phases in the creative process, many managers destroy good creative work by stinting on the resources they devote to the executional phase. But the public, the customers, are mostly unable to differentiate between the idea and its execution. On the contrary, if a basically poor idea is sufficiently well executed it will frequently achieve commercial success. Poor scripts brilliantly directed, poor commercials brilliantly produced, poor magazine articles brilliantly designed and illustrated – in each case the artifice may so enhance the original idea as to make it seem far better than it really is. The converse is rarely true. That is why it is so dangerous to pennypinch at the executional stage of a creative project, and managers who do so court disaster.

Another problem managers frequently face, at the border between idea and execution, emanates from creatives who try to do too much. This is very similar to the problem of creatives who try to work in too many styles. Some of the most massively talented creative people – Sir Lawrence Olivier and Orson Welles immediately spring to mind – have been able to master a wide range of disparate creative roles. Such multi-facetted talents are few and far between. Unfortunately many creatives, in more modest ways, try to tackle more than they are capable of. It is the manager's job to dissuade them.

In the creative industries specialization of labour applies with a vengeance. Most creatives, though they do not realize it, have exceptionally narrow creative abilities. In advertising, for example, few creators of press advertising are any good at television commercials; feature writers rarely make good fiction writers; designers are quite different from illustrators; fashion photographers can't shoot portraits; still photographers can't shoot movies. There are exceptions, but they are so infrequent as to be noteworthy. The creative manager should almost always urge creatives to stick to what they're best at, and to excel at the things they do well, rather than allow them to try and be jacks-of-all-trades.

Partly because of the high degree of specialization now needed in creative businesses, it is becoming increasingly necessary for creatives to work in groups, or teams. This is not a practice, or a way of working, which many creatives find easy. They aren't natural teamplayers. Independence is, as we saw in the last chapter, a basic trait. Wally Olins here summarizes both the need for intense specialization, and some of the problems it inevitably entails:

'We do huge, incredibly complex jobs. Nobody can do them alone, it's just not possible, there's just too much to do. One person can inspire the team, but one person can't do everything. The disciplines that are involved are very complex, and they're inter-related. There are project managers who look after the totality; there are graphic designers at various levels of seniority; there are architectural designers; there are print designers; there are typographical designers, and communications experts, and so forth and so on. Many of these people have little respect for the others. There are many aspects of a creative business where people don't respect each other's talents. They think the others get away with things, they think they're no bloody good, they think they let us all down – there's a lot of that. People within the organization think that some people are too precious, they take too long, they make too much of a meal of it, they think they're too bloody brilliant – all that kind of stuff.

'However, here they have to work in teams. They haven't any alternative. And usually when they work in teams even the most selfish of them, in the end, begins to recognize that they couldn't work outside a team. And if they antagonize the other members of the team they will find themselves in a worse position. So they begin to work better.'

The dynamics of social interaction in small groups, when people work together on related tasks, have been well-researched and documented.[4] Most of these studies have been carried out among general, non-creative groups, but it seems from Wally Olins' description of the process that in this respect at least, creatives' behaviour is far from atypical.

Interestingly, and perhaps surprisingly, one area of creative diversity that might have been expected to lead to a host of differing management problems does not appear to do so. Creatives in the different arts and disciplines – music, writing, design and so on – appear to share similar personality traits, and so to require similar styles of management. Admittedly data on the subject is still scarce, and future researchers may well find significant variances, but Wally Olins expresses the widely-held current view thus:

'I have quite a lot to do with writers, and quite a lot to do with architects, and with creative people in what you might call the graphic trades, and I don't see a vast difference between them emotionally.'

He goes on to say that because of their training, and because of the very different job functions they perform, there are sometimes clear *intellectual* differences between, eg, architects and illustrators. Similarly, David Puttnam feels that such differences as there are lie between originators (composers) and interpreters (instrumentalists). In other words, the differences are caused by the ways in which they do their work, rather than in their basic approach to the work itself.

On a broader scale, the varying ways in which the many creative industries are structured results in a range of different problems arising for the managers within each of them. The key differences, from industry to industry, result from two factors. First, the individual cost and number of the creative projects the organization handles. Second, the degree of day-to-day interaction between manager and creatives. The first is of far greater importance than the second, and experience proves that it is hardly understood at all – either by creatives or by managers; and least of all by governments, when they find themselves involved with the creative industries, as they so often do.

Put simply, it costs very little to produce a new book, whereas it costs a small fortune to produce a new film; new gramophone records can be, and are, launched on shoestring budgets, whereas new West End musicals can turn multi-millionaires into paupers overnight; small advertising leaflets can be printed for a pittance, television commercials can cost hundreds of thousands of pounds. These cost-per-project variations are of paramount importance in the creative industries, and the consequences that flow from them permeate many aspects of the management of creativity, as will be seen again and again throughout this book.

It has already been pointed out that commercial creativity inevitably involves a high degree of uncertainty, and therefore of risk. For most publishers, or record companies, the costs-per-project, and the commensurate financial risks, will be comparatively small. That is why publishers and record companies market so many titles and tunes. They can afford to spread their risks widely, knowing that many of their projects will fail, and hoping that enough will come good to bear the cost of the failures. However, any organization marketing a vast number of new products cannot afford to devote too much in the way of resources to any of them – not too much management time, not too much advertising or sales promotion, not too much quality control, little or no market research. Most of the individual projects do not warrant the time, and cannot carry the costs. As Paul Hamlyn entertainingly says:

'As a publisher you get a lot of "My dear Paul, my wife has written a book on Mongolian cooking. I'm sure . . ." You have to cope with it. I suppose I get a couple of dozen like that a week. So you become adept at saying "No". That is part of your skill. I have done it a couple of thousand times, I'm sure. And as a result one throws something good out mistakenly in some cases. Every publisher has lots of such stories.

'We're so big it would be impossible to watch everything. And it's not really my role. I'm a great believer in backing people up. But there are so many little pieces of the jigsaw, so many titles, so many authors, so many concepts, it's often very difficult. The best you can do is make sure everyone knows someone's watching them a bit.'

Similar in certain respects to books and records are weekly magazines, and even newspapers. Because each issue comes and goes quickly there is a limit to the amount of time and attention which can be applied to it. However, because magazines and newspapers enjoy 'brand loyalty' – which publishing houses and record companies have never achieved, to any degree – it may be worthwhile investing in the 'title', the implicit assumption being that the publication's format, and the consistency of its editorial control, will ensure that people who like one issue will also like the next, and the next. (A fascinating thesis could be written on the similarities and differences between 'branded' publications and branded consumer goods.)

Likewise popular fashion goods share certain similarities with books and records. They are produced in astonishing variety, enjoy a comparatively short sales life, and therefore cannot support heavy investment costs per garment. A massive number of quick, instinctive decisions have to be taken by the creatives and managers within the fashion industry, based on their judgment and experience, without the benefit of elaborate preparation or analysis.

At the other end of the spectrum is the blockbuster movie. With so much money at stake comparatively few films are made each year, and each gets star treatment from its makers. Only about 400 feature films are now made each year in Britain and the U.S. combined, compared with over 60,000 new books published in Britain alone. While the creatives working in most creative industries will be

expected to produce many different 'products' in a year, often working on several at the same time, in feature films it is not uncommon
to spend a year or longer working on the same project; but then the
costs, and the potential rewards, justify it.

In consequence, every tiny aspect of a major film will be pored
over and perused, questioned and qualified, dismembered and dis-
sected, broken down and totted up by a raft of executives all
employed to minimize the possibility of failure. As has already been
noted, they fail in this task with remarkable regularity. (It is only fair
to add that they have been fighting an uphill battle in a declining
industry for most of the past three decades. Perhaps the success
rate was higher in the early, boom days.) Inevitably, the costs and
concomitant risks force managers to try to play safe, to search desperately for proven creative formulae, to avoid taking creative risks, to
lean heavily on market research. The management disciplines could
hardly be more different from those in the low cost-per-project
creative industries. Not that every book is cheap to produce, nor
every film wildly expensive; but even extraordinarily expensive books
cost only a fraction of the price of a major movie, and even a cheap
feature film will cost several hundred thousand pounds. 'Today,' said
David Puttnam in a *Time* magazine profile, 'as I learned to my cost
at Columbia, almost every time you come up to bat you're making
a $20 million, or $30 million, or $50 million bet. That's not an
environment that encourages risk or adventurous creative decisions.'[5]

The television industry deploys a wide variety of low-cost to
high-cost programmes, and a corresponding variety of management
styles. In Britain the television companies – certainly the smaller
ones – operate more like book publishers than film companies. They
make a fair number of programmes, without too much fuss, allowing
the creatives fairly free rein. Here is Jeremy Isaacs describing how
he ran Channel 4:

'They (the creative people) had to persuade me that their vision
of the world was one that was worth backing. I didn't have to
agree with it to back it. Indeed, it would be impertinent for the
manager of an organization that broadcasts or produces a lot of
material to seek to identify himself or herself with every aspect
of it. I think that is an arrogant line for a manager to take. Even
if I did think something was wrong, if they could persuade me

that they were right then they were certainly allowed to go ahead.'

And here is Michael Grade on the same subject:

'My real job is to recognize the ideas that are dogs. That's basically what I do. I don't know for sure if something new is going to be successful, and if it is successful I have no way of knowing how successful it's going to be. I am really here to stop the ghastly ideas getting through. But I'm very persuadable. I look for obsession. I look for commitment. I look for them having thought the idea through. I want to be sure they understand any weaknesses in the idea. Then, if they still passionately want to do it, fine.'

Jeremy Isaacs contrasts this with American television, where the stakes are much higher, and management controls far tighter:

'If you compare British television with American television you are comparing, in the first instance, a system in which a very great deal of respect is paid to the creator's wishes and intentions. You do not attempt to force the writer and directors into a strait-jacket: "It's got to be like that otherwise we're not interested". On the contrary you say: "Hm, that's interesting, let's have a go. It ought to get quite a decent audience because it's on a really strong subject."

  'In America, exactly the opposite philosophy prevails: "Our examination of your project tells us that it's got an unhappy ending, and that means it's not going to get a big audience, and so irrespective of how much I admire the script, I have to tell you we can't do this." I once had an American executive tell me that what I was talking to him about was "too good". Such people are lobotomized. They're not using part of their minds. The result is a different sort of television. For the most part individuality, inspiration and creativity are mercilessly stamped out. It is in effect an industrial product, in which other considerations take priority over the creative instincts of the makers.'

Thus, the management systems which result from cost-per-project variances impinge heavily upon manager/creative relationships. This goes far to explain why creatives enjoy much greater freedom in Britain – a smaller market, with smaller costs, and smaller risks. It

equally explains, as a corollary, why the creative industries appear
to flourish more abundantly here. To quote from Sir Denis Forman's
MacTaggart lecture:

'In the matter of entertainment and the performing arts, we are
top dogs. British theatre, British television, British films have
built a respect for British values which has an incalculable effect
upon the psychology of the transatlantic relationship. It is the
last field of world leadership left open to us, and we neglect it
at our peril.'

The balance between management power and creative power – one
of the principal underlying themes of this book – is a delicate one.
In American creative industries management often exercises its authority a trifle too ham-fistedly, and many of the results are neither
attractive creatively nor all that successful commercially. However,
the difficulties involved in handling expensive, high-risk creativity
are by no means simple to resolve, as Jeremy Isaacs explains:

'One of the reasons why a lot of people who make huge success-
ess of managing commercial television, then make idiots of themselves in the film industry, is that the elements of safety and
risk are so totally different in each case. In British television, it
has simply been impossible to spend more on wrong creative
decisions than any ITV company could earn from advertising
revenue. So there was a huge degree of freedom within which
to take chances. They then went to the cinema where it's all
risk and no guarantee. Wrong decisions there, and it's disaster.'

The disaster is exaggerated by the fact that on television the multiplicity of programmes means that the occasional fiasco will soon be
lost and forgotten, whereas movies sink with about as much silence
and anonymity as the Titanic. The creatives however are not concerned with such differences. They simply want to get their work
produced, unimpeded and unhindered by management.

The final important area where the industry to industry variations influence management/creative relationships results from the
different levels of day-to-day involvement between them. To take
the extremes once again: having commissioned a book, the publisher
may have no further contact with the author for months or even
years, whereas a film producer and his director will work together
daily (and often nightly) throughout the duration of the production.

Inevitably, the closeness or distance of such relationships will effect the personal interactions between manager and creative, and will effect the ways in which they influence each other. To illustrate this point, consider the opinions of Christopher Bland, Michael Grade and Paul Hamlyn, quoted in Chapter 3, on the question of whether it is necessary for managers to like the creatives they deal with. They all say it isn't. But then none of them has to work in close proximity with individual creatives for protracted periods. David Puttnam, who, like any film producer, will find himself living and working cheek-by-jowl with the same creatives day and night, week after week, month after month, is far less sanguine about the problem:

'Working with people I dislike, even talented people, would destroy the atmosphere of teamwork, which is half of the pleasure of being in a creative business. I've had chunks of my life made miserable by other people's egos. I doubt if I'd work with them now. I don't think it's worth it.'

Sir Ralph Halpern, who also works closely with creatives on a continuous basis agrees:

'It is important that everyone mixes and gels, as the team synergy is important. No one individual is sufficiently important that their individual contribution is greater than the team contribution. It is unfortunate if a personality does not fit, but in that case it is unlikely that either the individual's or the group's output would be maximized.'

Frequency of contact not only effects personal relationships, it also effects the processes of briefing, amendment and rejection, to which we will return in Chapter 9. It is also, to some degree, the result of cost-per-project variations: the publisher cannot afford to spend much time with each of his authors, whereas the film producer needs to keep a tight grip on the project from beginning to end. Thus, there is much diversity, both of creativity itself and of the structures of the industries within which it flourishes. In this and the preceeding chapters we have concentrated on creativity, though the managers have reared their ugly heads from time-to-time, like interlopers. It is now time to look more closely at the managers' role in this labyrinthine jungle.

Footnotes

■

1. Clark, R. W. (1984) *Einstein: The Life and Times*, New York: Avon Books.
2. Bach, S. (1986) *Final Cut: Dreams and Disasters in the making of Heaven's Gate*, London: Jonathan Cape Limited.
3. Weisberg, R. W. (1986) *Op. cit.*
4. Argyle, M. (1973) *Social Interaction*, London: Tavistock Publications; Crosbie, P. V. (ed.) *Interaction in Small Groups*, New York: Macmillan Publishing Inc.
5. in *Time* magazine, 1 May, 1989.

5

The Role of the Manager

■

'Management is, all things considered, the most creative of all arts. It is the art of art. Because it is the organizer of talent,' says the eminent French thinker, Jean-Jacques Servan-Schreiber,[1] in a neat fusion of the twin themes of this book.

Not everyone would put management on quite so high a pedestal. Least of all the creatives who tend to feel that most of the executives whose job it is to manage them are at best worthy, and are often as not utterly incompetent. While David Puttnam, at the top of the ladder, believes it to be vital for managers and creatives to respect each others' abilities, lower down the rungs the relationships between managers and creatives are often hostile, suspicious and mutually disparaging. All of which results, in some measure, from managers' lack of understanding of exactly what their role should be. 'Your prime role as a manager,' says Jeremy Isaacs, 'is enabling creativity to fulfil itself. That's what you're there to do. You're not there to stop people being creative, you're there to help people be creative.'

As a succinct statement of the creative manager's job, that can hardly be bettered. Isaacs is fond of the concept of the manager as 'enabler'. Michael Grade uses an orchestral analogy, describing the manager as 'a conductor, with a lot of soloists'. David Puttnam prefers the word 'facilitator', which is almost a synonym of 'enabler'. He emphasizes that the facilitator must never become, or be seen to be, a 'servant' of the creatives:

'The manager is a facilitator, and I don't think the facilitator is a servant, but someone who makes things possible. If the manager sees himself as a servant – which is what happened to film producers in France, in the Sixties and Seventies – the whole damn thing goes down the sink eventually, because the film maker doesn't want a servant. He wants a colleague.'

For the colleague to carry out his enabling role effectively, he must fulfil four basic functions. He must recruit the right creatives for the job; motivate them to excel; ensure that they deliver at the right time and at the right cost; and get them to create the right creative product. We shall be exploring each of these functions in turn throughout the rest of the book. The creative manager's role is a demanding one.

In fact, there are not many individuals for whom the management of creative people is their full-time job. For most, it is only a part of their job, though an exceedingly important part. Perhaps that is why so little attention has been paid to the management of creativity in the past. The job titles of those involved vary from industry to industry: publisher, producer, controller, account executive, project manager, creative manager, planner (or any combination of these or similar words). Within the creative industries they all denote jobs which imply a close supervisory involvement with the creatives. Other management functions, not quite so close to the creative coalface, may also involve frequent interaction with creatives: chief executives and managing directors, production directors, marketing and brand managers, managing editors, programme controllers, co-ordinators, sales management, and even personnel. Finally – as creativity percolates into more and more aspects of business – a host of managers, with all kinds of functions and titles sporadically find themselves dealing with creatives on occasional jobs and projects.

A minority of those whose principal job is creative management begin their careers as creatives themselves, but decide at some stage that they prefer management to creativity. (Or maybe their superiors make the decision for them!) Having once worked as a creative has obvious advantages. It helps the manager to see the issues from both sides of the fence. As Jeremy Isaacs states:

'I have the insight of having been somebody himself who, by trying to make programmes as well as he possibly could, had to fight for the conditions in which it was possible to make them. I found out from being that side of the fence to what extent one had to live efficiently within whatever constraints were necessary, and to what extent one was sometimes entitled to say to the boss, "I've got to have a bit more room here."

Often the heads of creative departments will still be practising creatives, dividing their time, uncomfortably, between producing their own creative work and running their department. Trying to do two jobs at once, they rarely do either consumately well. Such individuals usually find it intensely difficult to settle down into full-time management roles. It is as though they had become addicted to creativity – addiction being the appropriate word, since they patently suffer withdrawal symptoms when they try to kick the creative habit.

It is fascinating, in passing, to note that the addictive power of creativity is not just a human phenomenon, but is a more basic animal instinct. In his book, *The Biology of Art*, Desmond Morris writes:[2]

'Apes, both young and adult, can become engrossed in picture-making to the point where they prefer it to being fed and will exhibit temper tantrums if they are stopped.'

Perhaps it is fortunate, then, that the majority of creative managers have never tried their hands at being creative, and are modest about their own creative talents. Indeed, many managers do not regard themselves or their jobs as creative and are uncomfortable with creative people, according to Stanley S. Gryskiewicz, director of Creativity Development at the Centre for Creative Leadership in America.[3] This, as we shall see in Chapter 11, is of some value as it enhances the excitement and pleasure that they get from working with creative people. But if managers have not worked closely with creatives early in their careers it is exceptionally rare for them to become good at it later in life.

Managers who have been brought up on a strict diet of production controllers, systems analysts, supplies officers and finance assistants, invariably choke on the indigestible ways of creatives if they first come across them in their forties or fifties. This is the source of a disastrous mistake often made by conglomerates and other large organizations when one of their 'creative subsidiaries' goes awry. They draft in a senior manager, with little or no experience of commercial creativity, to put things right. They then cannot understand why everything goes wrong. Steven Bach's *Final Cut* painfully demonstrates how poorly Transamerica Insurance understood the operations of its United Artists film-making subsidiary, hard as it tried. When UA ran into trouble, Transamerica appointed an intelligent, thoughtful, hard-working, conscientious and well-intentioned businessman to run it – a splendid chap in many respects, but with no knowledge of the movie business. Two years later United Artists collapsed.

One of the cardinal reasons why elderly novices cannot be expected to handle the role of creative manager successfully is that they cannot master the first of the essential basic functions: the recruitment of the right creatives. This is not an ability that can be acquired overnight, nor can it be rapidly absorbed on a management training course. To be good at it the manager must both enjoy and be perceptive about creativity. (And most of those who meet both criteria seek employment in the creative industry of their choice early on in life.) A newcomer, no matter how intelligent, thoughtful, hard-working, conscientious, well-intentioned and splendid, hasn't a cat in hell's hope of succeeding. Of course he can delegate the job – but in doing so he will delegate almost completely his power to control the creative output of the organization. To quote Jeremy Isaacs:

'In inviting them to do the job you've made your creative decision, which is which creator to work with. It's no use turning round afterwards and saying I didn't want this, I wanted something quite different.'

How does the creative manager carry out that basic decision, the recognition and employment of the right talented people? Without the right people the rest of the creative edifice can never be built. Creativity can be nurtured and developed – but it cannot be implanted or transformed. To return briefly to the argument in the last chapter:

'Creativity is like height, weight and strength. People vary considerably in these dimensions, but everybody has some height, some weight and some strength. Likewise, there is a certain amount of creativity in all of us, but some of us are obviously more creative than others.'[4]

If creativity were something that people had or did not have – like ten fingers or brown eyes – then it would be easy to divide the haves from the have-nots. Creativity is not like that. So the manager needs to be able to discern fine differences: differences of creative quality and differences of creative style. Every designer, or singer, or writer, applying for a job is likely to be quite good; but which will be right? (When, on one occasion, I questioned the first part of the thesis, I was sharply corrected by a headhunter, who said: 'Nobody thinks they can design, or sing, or write, if they can't do it *at all*. The people who apply for such jobs always have *some* aptitude. The eternal problem is, how much?')

Perhaps the simplest analogy is with tennis. Some people have no ball-sense whatsoever, and so find it hard to play at all; lots have sufficient ability to knock the ball about, but will never be any good; a few make excellent club players; fewer still are good enough to play for their county; a handful play for the country; and only the most exceptional play at Wimbledon. The extent to which training and environment effect this stratification is a subject to which we will return. But unless the individual has the essential natural talent – including the necessary ambition and determination – all the training in the world will be of no avail; and even the greatest players have utterly different styles.

So how can the manager assess creatives' talent and identify the right people for the right jobs? We have seen that intelligence is a far from perfect guide. It is often positively misleading, since people who are intelligent are usually articulate, confident and perform well in interviews. As a result, managers tend to react warmly to them, and reject inarticulate interviewees who may be much more talented. When recruiting creatives, verbal responses during the interview must not be overrated. The interviewer must keep in mind not only the comparative irrelevance of high intelligence, but also the personality traits associated with creativity. The applicant may well display insecurity, rebelliousness, stubborness and egotism – none of which are likely to enhance his interview performance. Hence, personal interviews – never wholly reliable as a means of assessing people's abilities – are especially unreliable in the case of creatives.

Nevertheless, there are things a manager can do to maximize the success rate. Be sure to keep in mind creatives' insecurities: be particularly attentive and sensitive to the individual; minimize interruptions; don't take telephone calls; don't rummage through the desk drawers, and don't open the post; give the interviewee the impression that for 10 or 15 minutes he is the most important person in the world. Some managers think it's smart to be calculatedly aggressive, to put respondents on their mettle, to run interviews as though they were pugilistic bouts. That may or may not be helpful in the recruitment of tough negotiators or sales representatives. In the recruitment of creatives it is almost guaranteed to be catastrophic.

New York University's Bernard Weiss lists the following common pitfalls to avoid during interviews with creatives:[5]

- Taking notes when the candidate is revealing sensitive, potentially damaging or personal information. It's best to wait for a change in the topic, or until the applicant is discussing something favourable or positive, before taking notes.

- Asking questions likely to be answered 'yes' or 'no'. With less verbal persons you need a list of leading questions, such as 'What prompts you to consider leaving your present job?' or 'What five things have you done that you are most proud of?'

- Conducting an inquisition. Although the interview is being conducted at your request, your guest should feel involved in a discussion, not an enquiry.

Creative tests, of which there are many, are useful for establishing whether otherwise ordinary people do or do not have any creative spark, but are no help whatsoever in assessing the degree of talent in reasonably (or highly) creative individuals. Tests which measure an awareness of good design have been shown to be 'the most powerful tests yet discovered as a predictor of creative potential in any field of endeavour'.[6] But once again they cannot identify fine differences of quality, let alone differences in style.

In any event it is rarely possible to get senior creatives to take creativity tests. Fortunately this matters little since, reflecting the above research findings, management studies have shown that the most reliable way to identify an individual's *prospective* creative performance is through his *previous* creative performance. The best way to tell if he will do well in future is to see what he has done well in the past. In assessing past performance the manager is greatly aided by creatives' predeliction for fame. As creatives are personally identified with their work, it is comparatively easy for the manager to spot and keep methodical track of talented people. Anyway, he needs to track precisely who is producing what in order to keep fully abreast of current trends and fashions.

Unfortunately, no rules can be defined which will readily tell a manager how to spot talent. That seems itself to be an inborn talent, as leading creative managers recognize:

> 'I'm not terribly creative myself, but I do think I'm good at spotting creative people. I don't think there is any real training for it. It's the nose, the hunch. I'm a great believer in that. And if you have the nose, all-in-all you get it right.' (Paul Hamlyn)

> 'I think that I have a creative instinct. I think that I have an inner eye.' (Wally Olins)

Nose, eye, instinct or hunch can all be honed and sharpened with experience. For example, cynical though it may sound, it pays to be suspicious. Individuals' output may be branded with the names, but that by no means proves it is all their own work. Creatives are just as prone to plagiarize, fib or exaggerate their contribution to anything that has been successful as the rest of humanity (if not more so). Moreover, creatives frequently work well within a particular team or ambience, but fail as soon as they venture outside. They themselves may genuinely not appreciate their dependence on a set of colleagues, but the manager must. One of the commonest pitfalls is not to allow for the transitory effect upon an inferior talent of working with a brilliant team. Just as in tennis, or in any other sport, everyone plays better alongside better players. It is the same with creativity. The dilemma for the manager is to decide exactly how much (or how little) of the superior talent has been absorbed; to what extent the prospective employee has been permanently improved by the association. Thus, some average cameramen shoot marvellously when inspired by great directors, but are lost when left to themselves. Others learn from the directors, and go on to become fine directors themselves.

Having spotted the talent, the next hurdle is to recruit it. (In most creative businesses this is largely outside the control of any but the most senior management.) Good creative people are always in demand, and know they are. So for them job selection is a two-way process. This is always the case with good people, to some degree; with good creative people the degree is very much greater than average. They will be just as anxious as their prospective employer to ensure that the job is right for them. Many a manager has emerged from interviewing a creative wondering dazedly who was choosing whom. Though no statistics exist, it is a safe bet that creatives are more prone than others to reject job offers – even after lengthy and detailed negotiations. Their main asset being their creative talent, they are anxious (albeit instinctively) to ensure that that asset is invested to their advantage, as wisely and well as possible.

Most of the factors which influence a creative's job choices will be the same as would influence anyone else. However, two factors hold a much greater significance for creatives, and may relegate even such a prime consideration as remuneration to third or fourth place. First, creatives are always intensely concerned about the reputation of any employer; and second, they are concerned about whether the employer will provide them, personally, with opportunities to produce outstanding work. The two are interlocked; and both are embedded in the creative personality and its intricacies.

It is doubtful whether employees in any other type of industry spend as much time discussing the merits and demerits of the companies in their field. To outsiders, overhearing creatives in pubs and at parties, the level of their interest will sound veritably obsessive. The creatives will debate endlessly whether architect A's star is rising, while architect B is on the wane; whether advertising agency P is the current hotshop, while Q has passed its peak; whether record company X has all the newest sounds, while Y seems to be going M-O-R and Z hasn't had a good group in years.

In *Final Cut*,[7] Steven Bach relates how United Artists put a massive effort into improving its creative image, not with the public, but within the movie business. It was because UA was scared of falling out with director Michael Cimino – then a hot creative property – that they allowed him to overspend grossly on Heaven's Gate and thus drive the company towards oblivion. Why were they so scared? Because if Cimino had quit it would have been detrimental to their reputation as creative movie-makers. Why did that matter? Because without a creative reputation the company would not be able to recruit top stars, top writers, top directors, top talent of any kind. It's the same in advertising, publishing, fashion, architecture . . . the creatives all want to work with the companies with the top creative reputations. They may well accept a lot less money, and even lousy working conditions, to do so.

They are not altogether wrong. As we have noted, working with other top creatives will burnish their talent. Even if it does so only temporarily, it will provide them with the opportunity to produce work which will enhance their reputation for the future. If it does so permanently, the value of their talent will be increased for good. The best companies get the best opportunities, and so they produce the best work, and so they are able to recruit the best staff, and so they continue to get the best opportunities. The system would be eternally self-perpetuating, but for the fact that even the brightest creative stars eventually fade. An incidental, but important, by-product of the willingness of creatives to accept lower payment from companies with high creative reputations is that such companies can, and do, keep their personnel costs lower, and hence their profitability higher. This effect has been clearly noticeable, for example, among the publicly quoted advertising agencies.

If a company does not have a strong creative reputation it will nonetheless need to convince prospective employees of its ability to provide them with the opportunity to produce outstanding work. The employee will be well aware that the organization is not crowded with talent. In the unlikely event that the employee hasn't noticed, he will have been told about it by creative friends, and will be concerned about the effect upon his own reputation of working for an organization with a poor creative image. The employer may be able to turn this to advantage, by pointing out to the potential recruit that here is a unique personal opportunity to improve the quality of the work, and thus to build the company's creative image. ('After all, if you're working at XYZ you'll just be one fish in a crowded creative pond; here you'll have the pond all to yourself, and any improvements will be seen to be your own . . .') Having made such a promise, the creative manager will need to be seen to be working hard to make it come true. Talented creatives are never short of job offers, and competitors will circle over an unhappy one like birds of prey inspecting a tasty morsel.

None of this should come as a surprise. Creatives' attitudes to their jobs, and thus to their employers, can be deduced from their personality traits. They are people who are prepared to be judged by their output, so the quality of their output matters intensely to them, and they recognize that this is in large measure dependent upon the quality of their employer. They are egotistical and insecure, both of which characteristics will be massaged if they work for organizations with high reputations. They are stubborn and rebellious, both of which will be better understood and accepted within creative, rather than uncreative, organizations. They are perfectionist, and so job satisfaction is of great importance to them. All of which explains why the good ones are so picky about accepting jobs.

Naturally their attitude to the job will vary if it doesn't involve full-time employment. If the creative, or maybe his consultancy, is being employed on a freelance or project basis, to carry out an assignment which will not last too long, he may well be less pernick-ety. After all, the next job may be better. But even in this situation, creatives will be well aware that carrying out too many hack jobs will harm their reputation, lower their value, and therefore their prices, and won't be much fun anyway. To counter this possibility, particu-larly when getting started, talented freelance creatives often charge lower fees for the jobs they really want – a point to which we'll return when covering the subject of cost control in Chapter 5.

On the subject of employing freelances and consultants, one final important point. In no other industries are lawyers busier, or happier, or remunerated more handsomely; in no other industries is there more litigation between employers and employed. In his sensational exposé of the seamier side of Hollywood, *Indecent Exposure*,[8] author David McClintick states: 'The entertainment industry functions in a jungle of contracts'. The same is true of all the creative industries. Partly it is because of the amorphous nature of creativity, which makes it so difficult to say whether or not the creatives have really delivered the goods they promised; partly it is due to the complexities of copyright law; partly it is because remuneration packages are structured in complicated ways; partly it is because creatives' innate rebelliousness makes them litigious; partly it is because creative managers too often fail to tie up loose ends as tightly as they should. Whatever the reasons, there can be no doubt that one of the key responsibilities of every manager who employs creatives – particularly on an *ad hoc* or project basis – is to draw up the most precise specification possible for each assignment. Lawyers and legal documentation are unavoidable, even though their powers to control creatives are limited.

(In the 1970s I ran a 'Poem of the Month Club'. I never expected it to be the most lucrative venture in the history of commerce, but it was good fun. Many of the world's finest and most famous poets contributed poems. From the start my partner warned that water-tight contracts would have to be drawn up with each contributor because, he said, world famous poets were up to even more chicanery, and were even less reliable, than businessmen. He was right.)

For many managers of creativity, the job of finding and recruiting creatives will not be one of their responsibilities. It will be the responsibility of the head of the company, or the head of the department. They will be expected to work with the creatives they are given, so to speak, and will only be able to change them by making an inordinate fuss. And maybe not even then.

It is the job of all managers, however, to motivate and control 'their' creatives. That is the subject matter of the rest of this book. But it is vital to emphasize, before we move on, that the manager's responsibilities are not solely, or even principally, to the creatives. As has already been stressed, the manager is the interface between creativity and other people. The other people may be customers or clients, or colleagues within the organization, or the public at large. To all these people the manager, and not the creatives, will be the person responsible for delivering the creative product to them. So his role is not merely to butter-up the creatives. If that were the job it would be laughably easy. But as Michael Grade states:

> 'As I keep reminding people here, ten times a week, it's the viewer who's sovereign, not the producer, not the head of department, not the commissioning editor, not me. We're all here to serve the audience, and nothing must get in the way of that.'

In the fashionable, Gadarene rush to encourage creativity, those few management theorists who have written about the subject appear to have forgotten that the role of the manager is not simply to keep the creatives cheerful but, as Christopher Bland puts it, 'to create an environment in which creative people can enjoy themselves – without running riot'. Or as Jeremy Isaacs spells it out more fully:

> 'The problem of employing creative people in an organization which in any sense is an industrial one is that their creativity sometimes needs to be tempered to the constraints within which the organization is able to work . . . they have to be creative within the budget that you can afford and on a timetable that enables you to plan.'

The manager, in other words, must ensure that the work is finished on time, and within its budget, and that it meets the requirement of the organization – whether expressed as a tight brief, or simply in terms of aims and objectives. Having found the right creatives for the job, the manager must motivate them, control them and ensure that they deliver a final product which is superior to that which they might have produced on their own, and – much more importantly, as we live in a competitive world – is superior to that which any other creative organization would have produced.

The manager must always feel powerful enough, and confident enough, to question and criticize the work of creatives – however difficult that may be with creatives who may be leaders in their field. Nor, if they are wise, will talented creatives want to work with managers whom they can dominate. To quote David Puttnam:

'It is as important for the manager to respect the artist as for the artist to respect the manager. If either gets hopelessly out of kilter, lousy work is the result.'

'How many times,' asks Anne Billson, 'does one get the feeling, watching a film nowadays, that the director could have done with someone who might have given him a slap on the wrist, someone who might have said, "Hang on, *this* is what the public wants," someone with enough confidence in his own opinions and judgment to challenge the maestro at work?'[9]

Is it only the idiosyncracies of the creative personality that make the role of the creative manager so difficult? Not at all: it is the nature of creativity. The manager wants the creatives to produce something wonderful, something better than the competition, something that the customers will like and want and be willing to pay for. Yet at the outset, neither the manager nor the creatives have any clear idea at all of what exactly it is that they're going to end up with. As David Puttnam puts it:

'It is difficult to be precise with regard to the end product, because of the imprecision of describing it. When you start out you are describing something amorphous, which you are encouraging or asking them to create. That is a very specific management problem.'

That initially amorphous nature of the creative product is an issue to which we shall return frequently in the following chapters.

Footnotes

■

1. Rooks, R. (1981) 'Creativity and Conformity: Finding the Balance', *Management World*.
2. Morris, D. (1962) *Op. cit.*
3. in Necton, S. (1985) 'How to Spark New Ideas', *Nation's Business*: US Chamber of Commerce.
4. Badawy, M. K. (1986) *Op. cit.*
5. Weiss, B. (1986) 'Hiring Creative People', *Personnel Administrator*: American Society for Personnel Administration.
6. Gough, H. G. 'Identifying the Creative Man', *Journal of Value Engineering*: vol. 2 no. 4.
7. Bach, S. (1986) *Op. cit.*
8. McClintick, D. (1982) *Indecent Exposure*, New York: William Morrow & Company Inc.
9. Leff, L. J. *The Times*, 15 April, 1989: quoted from Anne Billson's review of 'Hitchcock and Selznick'.

6

Motivating Creativity

■

Managing creativity is not unlike driving a car in town: bursts of acceleration, frequent braking, unforseeable hazards, numerous changes of direction and a high risk of accident. Rarely is it like driving on a deserted motorway, demanding only attentiveness and a gentle nudge of the wheel from time to time. In this chapter we will be analyzing the means of acceleration.

All good management involves leadership. The leadership of creatives is particularly difficult because they are prone to disdain leaders. They will admire tremendously, and may try to emulate, other creatives. But managers, lacking overt creative talent, can find it hard to win their esteem. Outside of the creative industries, in the great mass of boss/subordinate relationships, subordinates accept instructions because they know that is how organizational hierarchies function, and they know that organizational hierarchies are an unavoidable fact of life. Few creatives accept that organizational hierarchies are an unavoidable fact of life. If a manager is to lead them he must get their respect, and to get their respect he must earn it. It won't be bestowed upon him merely because of his status in the hierarchy.

Throughout history thinkers have debated whether leaders are born or made. Indubitably some individuals have the quality called *charisma*. ('Charisma', incidentally, a much misused word, literally means 'a gift from God': something you are born with, not something that can be acquired.) Charismatic leaders, then, are born with some peculiar quality which makes people follow them. Whether charisma is a unique quality which differentiates those who have it from those who don't, or whether it is a quality which almost everybody has in some degree (like creativity) is an issue which has never been resolved. In any event, whether somebody has charisma or not, he can unquestionably acquire basic leadership skills, just as quite average army officers can be taught to be highly effective leaders in battle.

Charles Handy, visiting professor at the London Business School, provided a useful definition of the nature of managerial leadership in his book, *The Age of Unreason*.[1] 'A leader shapes and shares a vision which gives point to the work of others,' Handy says, and goes on to define five key aspects of successful leadership:

- The leader's vision must be different.

- The leader's vision must make sense to others.

- The leader's vision must be understandable.

- The leader must live the vision.

- The leader must remember that the vision will remain a dream without the work of others.

Charles Handy's general definition almost exactly matches Jeremy Isaacs' description of the role of the creative manager:

'The absolutely critical thing is that you have to make clear to them that you can offer them a vision of your intention in running the organization which they can realize matches theirs, that you believe in what they believe in. It is not done by making great speeches. It's done by knowing what you want to do yourself, and being able to communicate it simply, friendlily, directly. They don't have to feel you share their tastes. They have to feel that you have room in your pantheon for their own expression of their particular vision.'

In order to motivate the work of others, especially when the others are creatives, the leader must set them challenges; make them stretch themselves. As we have seen, new things rarely come into existence without a struggle. One of the paradoxes of creativity is that creatives desperately want to create yet often have to be forced to do so. (This is not such uncommon human behaviour: many sportsmen desperately want to improve their performance yet still need tough trainers to bully them into it.) This is how David Puttnam sees it:

'Very good creative work falls into the area of problem solving.

All you've got to do is to set the problem. You set the challenge, you set the objective, and the creative person can function within those parameters.'

Setting the challenge leads to the subject of briefing, which will be discussed fully in the next chapter. But there are other, equally important aspects of challenge: criticizing poor work and the maintenance of high standards. Managers who approve all the creative work shown to them soon lose credibility and respect. All creatives know their work is patchy, much as it galls them to acknowledge it; all creatives know there are times when they need to be pushed, even if they'll never admit it. It is something about which Puttnam feels especially keen:

'The demand for excellence is vital. For creative people competence is only acceptable as a point of departure, *en route* towards excellence or even greatness. Never allow competence to be an end result. The first idea they have is a point of departure, seldom an answer. The manager mustn't allow it to be an answer, because they might start to believe they're a genius.

'In addition, the manager mustn't allow emotional creativity to detract from the value of sheer professionalism. The manager must have a very definite and well-understood demand for professionalism, and not allow the notion of genius to detract from his day-to-day insistence on professionalism'.

David Puttnam's empirical finding is confirmed by Professor William B. Kirkwood, of East Tennessee State University:[2]

'Research on how people solve tough, unfamiliar problems suggests that the first solution considered is rarely as original or as useful as the second or third. Why? The first idea that comes to mind will usually be the most obvious. Of course, if the problem we face is routine, this may be good enough. But if the task is difficult and unusual, obvious answers won't work. Unless we get past the obvious, we are unlikely to meet the challenge.'

Tim Bell believes that, in advertising at least, this is an area where managers are unacceptably lax:

'One thing that's wrong with the advertising business is that (managers) are frightened. So although a very large number of the ideas the creatives come up with aren't any good, people don't have the guts to say "that's rubbish". So the creatives get an easy ride – which really isn't good for them, or for their creativity.'

In other words, just as creatives demand perfectionism in themselves, they demand it in their managers. Inevitably this leads to conflicts, because creatives' notions of the perfect rarely equate with managers' notions of the perfect. If the conflicts are repeated and incessant, they will not be able to work together: their styles are too mismatched. But managers never lose the respect of creatives by complaining about their work not being good, original or creative enough. Managers only lose the creatives' respect when they complain about their work being too different, or radical, or saying that it doesn't follow established principles and guidelines. Then the creatives know that their very existence is being threatened, because they are being called upon not to create, but to repeat. All of which explains why the rejection of creative work is a matter which must be handled with care. (This will be covered in detail in Chapter 9.)

While leadership and challenges activate creatives' perfectionism, to boost their motivation it is also necessary to massage their insecurities and egotism. (Robert Jacoby – then the diminutive but exceedingly powerful chairman of Ted Bates Inc., the second largest advertising agency in the world – once said to me: 'If people knew how much time I spend around here massaging people's egos they'd think I was crazy.')

Massage can be given in a variety of ways, though all add up to much the same thing:

'Lots of cuddles. Very Important. Verbal cuddles and physical cuddles. But certainly lots of verbal cuddles.' (Paul Hamlyn)
'You have to flatter their egos. It is an enormous process of charming them, persuading them, treating them a bit like naughty schoolchildren. Of course I could mention creatives who aren't like that, but even in those there is still a little touch of the petulant ego.' (Tim Bell)
'You have to have an attitude which is like a parent to an adolescent. You've got to be nice and you've got to keep on explaining. It's very trying on the nerves.' (Wally Olins)
'They require constant reassurance and encouragement.' (Sir Ralph Halpern)

'You endlessly have to cheer them up, to reassure and flatter them, and to establish a relationship of trust and encouragement, which is sometimes necessary to put them to work.' (Jeremy Isaacs)

It must be added that good managers are not unsympathetic to the reasons for creatives' need for such flattery – as Jeremy Isaacs, for example, explains:

'It is all necessary because they give something that drains, they give more of themselves than other people give in their daily working lives, and therefore are entitled to that little bit of extra support.'

And Sir Ralph Halpern concurs:

'Creative people's ability to create is heavily dependent on their belief in themselves. It is essential that management recognizes this and provides the necessary encouragement.'

(Similar views are expressed by Michael Grade and David Puttnam, in the discussion of the creative personality in Chapter 3.)

To motivate creatives, managers must also provide the right environment, both behaviourally and – as far as is within their power – physically. In behavioural terms, here are nine simple rules which can help managers win creatives' support and enthusiasm:

- Absorb their risks – managers who encourage creativity must willingly and publicly take their share of the blame if things go wrong.

- Stretch organizational regulations – though managers should not normally disregard rules and policies, they must know when these need to be more honoured in the breach than in the observance.

- Be comfortable with half-developed ideas – it should not be necessary for every 't' to be crossed and every 'i' to be dotted before an idea is given consideration; and creatives must have confidence that the manager can really understand and appreciate ideas at an early stage of gestation.

- Make quick decisions – managers who ho-hum and sit on the fence when shown creative ideas soon stop being shown creative ideas.

- Don't dwell on mistakes – mistakes are an inherent part of the creative process. Managers should ensure that creatives learn from experience, but not make them wallow in it – 'I told you so' is a particularly unappealing phrase to creatives.

- Be a good listener – creatives generally love to talk about their work, and managers have to love (or learn to love) to listen.

- Provide lots of feedback – creatives are always eager for evaluation of their work, and since real results are often long delayed (and even then not necessarily precise) the manager must provide as much encouraging data, along the way, as possible.

- Accept trivial foibles – we have already seen that creatives are not quite the same as everyone else; allowing them a few innocent quirks will stress your acceptance of non-conformity.

- Defend them against attackers – in all creative businesses, creatives are subject to frequent, and often unjustified, criticism: the manager must speak up, and be heard to speak up, loudly and boldly on their behalf.

If these are all positive ways to encourage creativity, here are 57 not quite lighthearted ways to block it, from Michael Badawy's *How to Prevent Creativity Mismanagement*:[3]

A good idea but . . .
Against company policy.
Ahead of the times.
All right in theory.
Be practical.
Can you put it into practice?
Costs too much.
Don't start anything yet.
Have you considered . . .
I know it won't work.
It can't work.
Too many projects already.
It doesn't fit human nature.

The client won't understand
The timing is wrong.
There are better ways.
They won't go for it.
Too clever.
Too hard to administer.
Too hard to implement.
Too late.
Too much paperwork.
Too old-fashioned.
Too soon.
We have been doing it this way for a long time and it works.

It has been done before.
It needs more study.
It's not budgeted.
It's not good enough.
It's not part of your job.
Let me add to that . . .
Let's discuss it.
Let's form a committee.
Let's make a survey first.
Let's not step on toes.
Let's put if off for a while.
Let's sit on it for a while.
Let's think it over for a while.
Not ready for it yet.
Of course it won't work.
Our plan is different.
Some other time.
Surely you know better.
That's not our problem.
The boss won't go for it.

We haven't the manpower.
We haven't the time.
We're too big.
We're too small.
We've never done it that way.
We've tried it before.
What bubble-head thought that up?
What will the customers think?
What you're really saying is . . .
Who else has tried it?
Why hasn't someone suggested it before if it's a good idea?

So far we have been considering behavioural rules, both positive and negative, and the behavioural environment. Questions concerning physical environment are far more difficult to answer at all dogmatically. The physical environment will obviously vary greatly from industry to industry. Films are shot on sets and on location; television programmes are made in studios and on location; many writers work at home; musicians work in rehearsal rooms; photographers and journalists roam around, and so on. Sir Ralph Halpern suggests that this is an area where different types of creatives may have quite different needs:

'A clothes designer is likely to want a bright, vibrant environment, with lots of colours and clothes around to stimulate their creativity. A writer, on the other hand, may prefer the peace of a study and require no other stimulus. In each case the personal requirements to induce creativity would need to be provided.'

Although it is universally agreed that creatives are particularly sensitive to their physical environment, many small creative companies operate successfully from shambolic, over-crowded and dilapidated offices, and many creatives seem to like it that way. Here, for example, is Paul Hamlyn describing his company's move to the splendidly elegant Bibendum building in South Kensington:

'I fought hard to get this building because I believe this is the sort of environment that creative people can work best in. But a lot of them hate it.'

And Christopher Bland, on the same theme, says:

'Many great publishers and many great editors have worked in higgledy-piggledy offices stuffed with books and crowded with paper. Offices which have never seen the hand of a design consultant anywhere near them. Take Century Hutchinson. Hutchinson used to work in a thoroughly poky environment, but when Century Hutchinson joined together they moved into rather more spacious, open plan, modern, comfortable premises. I'm not sure that people are working necessarily either better or worse. It would be difficult to prove, either way.'

However, to some creative organizations – particularly architectural and design consultancies – their physical and structural environment is of the greatest importance. Wally Olins believes this to be so for his company:

'The environment is key in all this, the physical atmosphere in the building. We don't want a situation emerging where people are secretly working for days or weeks, nights or weekends, on a project which, when they present it, is quite clearly nonsensical . . . The building is the key to the way we run the business. Everybody is accessible. The chairman's office is open plan, in the centre of the work-space. If I'm not in it and somebody wants to use it, they use it. This is done (a) because we want to be accessible, and (b) because we want to show people we have respect for them as human beings.'

A few advertising agencies share Olins' attitudes, but they are a minority. Most are concerned with the cosmetic appearance of their reception and their important conference rooms, but otherwise work in fairly conventional offices – like the majority of other creative businesses.

Motivation is a forward-looking process. The degree to which any individual is motivated to carry out a task depends upon the perception that carrying out the task will help him achieve the results he desires. So it might seem strange that in this discussion of motivation one all-important word has not yet been mentioned: money. There are two reasons. First, creatives' attitude to their remuneration is not terribly different from other peoples'. Second, as has already been indicated, insofar as they are different at all, creatives' attitudes tend to diminish the importance of remuneration as a motivating factor. That is not to say creatives are not interested in money, far from it. They most certainly are.* However, there appears to be no correlation whatsoever between the money they are paid and the resulting quality of their work. Unlike piece-workers, they cannot be incentivized to work harder by being paid more; their productivity cannot be geared to their wages. The best creatives, as has been said, get the most money; but it happens that way round. The money is paid to them for their talent, not to motivate them to do better.

'Ironically, the reward goldcollar workers want most – even more than money – is peer recognition,' claims Mark L. Goldstein, and this is confirmed by other research which has been carried out to discover which factors are most significant in stimulating creativity among engineers and scientists (not, admittedly 'artistic' creatives, among whom no such research has apparently been undertaken). The most important factors are, in descending order:[4]

- Recognition and appreciation
- Freedom to work in areas of greatest interest
- Contact with stimulating colleagues
- Encouragement to take risks

* 'It is generally thought,' quipped the brilliant American advertising agency chief, Howard Gossage, 'that artists are interested in art. Nothing could be further from the truth. Artists are interested in money. It's the rest of us who are interested in art.' Gossage obviously shared Dr Johnson's unromantically mercenary view of the creative process (see page 8).

The lowest-rated factors, also in descending order, are:

- Non-conformity tolerated
- Opportunity to work alone rather than on a team
- Monetary rewards
- Criticism by supervisors or associates
- Creativity training programmes
- Regular performance appraisals.

Many of these points have been discussed above – though it is interesting to note how little value is put upon both training and appraisal. However, it seems clear, if the research has any validity, that motivating creativity amongst scientists and engineers is different from doing so among commercial creatives in at least one crucial respect. Among commercial creatives the single most important factor is the perceived opportunity to fulfil themselves. This need for self-fulfilment derives from their egotism, their perfectionism, their insecurity and their craving for fame. It explains why, as we shall see in Chapter 9, they take criticism of their work so badly. To the manager it is the master key, with which all of their creative energies can be unlocked. As Jeremy Isaacs explains:

'The most important way in which creative people are distinguished is by their single-mindedness, their belief that the beauty of a project, the excellence of a script or a film, has to be realized to the ultimate degree.'

To return to Isaacs' definition of the creative manager as an 'enabler', if the manager enables them to do the work they want to do, to fulfil themselves, to create work of which they are proud and which others admire, the creatives will work tirelessly in his service; and they will fight to do so. Here is David Puttnam's excellent analysis of the question:

'How do you motivate creative people? This is the crux of the issue. Give them confidence. Allow them to believe in themselves. Create an atmosphere where there is a sense that anything is possible, great work is possible. Part and parcel of that freedom is to be a master of technique. So a large part of motivating creative people is to train them properly, so they have so much confidence in their technique – like a good driver behind the wheel – that they don't have to think about it, they need only think about moving on. A lot of people spend their lives obsessed by the inadequacies of their technique, and that is a tremendous stumbling block. I'm a great believer in training, and the mentor ethos.

'You also need the environment. You can be a brilliant darts player, and you can slog away in the pub day after day, but if you've not got anyone there nurturing you, correcting your errors, someone to criticize your play and encourage you, you'll hardly improve.

'You need natural talent, hard work and an environment that demands excellence. If you lack any one of these three, you'll probably be back to square one.'

Sir Ralph Halpern likewise views the manager's role as that of an 'enabler':

'To enable the free flow of creative thought, it is essential that the manager provide a working environment that is not restrictive or stifling, and allows creatives to discuss their ideas freely without fear of being ridiculed.'

Lastly, on the subject of motivation, it is vital to remember that it is a continuous, day by day process, not something that can be switched on with a counterfeit smile whenever the manager happens to remember. This is true of all management, but is especially true of the management of insecure and often prickly creatives. So here are four precepts to keep in mind when dealing with creatives every day of the year:

- Search for the praiseworthy – as Kenneth Blanchard and Spencer Johnson put it in their classic bestseller, *The One Minute Manager*:[5] 'Catch them doing something right'. Search for the opportunities and they will be found.

- Praise the praiseworthy – maybe it is traditional British reticence (Americans don't seem to suffer from the same disability) but many managers find it embarrassing to pay compliments when work is well done. When dealing with creatives this is simply disastrous. Don't overdo it – if you gush too much and praise them too often or too easily, you will depreciate the value of the praise; nor, as you might hope, will it win you their affection. Occasional, enthusiastic and sincere praise is infinitely more valuable than incessant and over-enthusiastic slaps-on-the-back.

- Reprimand rapidly – reprimands are as intrinsic to effective motivation as praise, provided they are accepted and understood by the creative concerned; this is why it is crucial not to delay them.

- Be specific – whether praising or blaming, concentrate on the particular work involved, and let the creative know as precisely as possible what is good/bad about it.

And as a final footnote, never forget that one of the best motivators of all is to make creative work fun. Some psychologists have claimed that having a good sense of humour is an essential ingredient in the creative personality – but that is far from proven. What is beyond question is that many creatives like to lark about when working together. It relieves tensions, generates enthusiasm and relaxes the mind. Wise managers let it happen.

With so much motivation the creatives should by now be raring to accelerate away: but unfortunately we are not yet ready to start moving.

Footnotes

■

1. Handy, C. (1989) *The Age of Unreason*, London: Hutchinson.
2. Kirkwood, W. B. (1983) 'The Search for Good Ideas', *Supervisory Management*: The American Management Association.
3. Badawy, M. K. (1986) *Op. cit.*
4. *Ibid.*
5. Blanchard, K. and Johnson, S. (1983) *The One Minute Manager*, London: Fontana.

7

A Brief on Briefing

■

Most of the first half of this book has been concerned with creativity and its encouragement. As background, it has been possible to draw upon a number of psychological and management studies, albeit not many. However, such is the universal enthusiasm for maximizing creativity that virtually nobody has done any work on how to control it. Yet the essence of commercial creativity, as opposed to pure art, is that it must operate within disciplines. (Many would argue that the same is true of pure art, but that is not our concern.) Every manager of creativity knows that his job comprises restraint as well as encouragement: the brake as well as the accelerator. And the first place to apply the brake (if this isn't too creative a thought) is before the journey begins.

It is all but impossible to stress too strongly the importance of briefing. Nothing causes more ill-will between creatives and managers than the waste of time, effort, resources and imagination which are the direct and unavoidable consequences of inadequate briefing. Money is lost, tempers frayed; mutual respect dwindles to nil. Invariably each side blames the other. The managers insist that the creatives failed (or didn't even bother to try) to understand the brief, while the creatives insist that the brief was too vague, or incomprehensible, or downright wrong. Invariably the work has to be done again, and maybe again, in ever greater haste. The organization incurs increased costs, other work gets delayed, clients and customers wonder whether to take their business elsewhere, and sometimes do so. There can be no question, to adapt the old military maxim, that time spent on briefing is seldom wasted.

Before even starting to brief the creatives, however, the manager must establish in his own mind what the creatives are required to do. It may well be, as we shall see, that part of their task will be to help the manager define the problem. So long as the manager makes it clear, that is a perfectly acceptable preliminary task. The manager will still need to do all the necessary homework beforehand. Remembering the manager's role as interface, he may need to find out what the clients or customers expect the creative work to achieve; what the organization wants the creative work to achieve – in terms of sales or audience levels; whether there are areas of creativity that must be avoided, or must be included. If it is impossible to stress too strongly the importance of briefing, it is almost equally impossible to stress too strongly the need for the manager to dig deep, leave no stone unturned and find out everything he can about the project before the briefing begins.

Briefings can be either written, or verbal, or both. (Some managers have strong views on this issue, to which we'll return.) The objectives of all briefings are two-fold. First, to let the creatives know as exactly as possible what is required and to encourage them to excel. Second, to let them know as exactly as possible of any specifications or constraints within which they must work. To achieve the first objective the brief must inspire, enthuse and intrigue; the creatives must be convinced that the project is in some way special, exciting, worthwhile. So the brief itself must be imaginative, stimulating, involving. Dull briefs produce dull work. All of which is fraught with difficulties because, as David Puttnam put it earlier, 'when you start out you are describing something amorphous, which you are encouraging or asking them to create'. The second objective is similarly fraught because many specification details are often unknown at the start of a project, and may be intricately inter-dependent ('. . . if it's going to be printed in six colours it will need to be on this quality of paper, which in turn means using that kind of ink, which in turn . . .') In practice briefings can be divided into two stages:

Stage I
Briefings in which the objectives and constraints are stated in broad and general terms.

Stage II
Briefings in which the objectives and constraints are defined precisely and specifically.

There is no sharp dividing line between the two stages, and unless they abort early on, most creative projects shade from Stage I to Stage II as they progress. As they near completion there may well be a welter of tiny briefings – detailed changes, amendments to the specification, etc. – which are hardly even recognized as such.

Simplified for the sake of clarity, examples of Stage I briefings might be:

'We need a new light entertainment TV serial, aimed at the affluent young'.

'We need some cheap and cheerful summer fabric designs, for middle-aged housewives'.

'We're looking for a format for a new men's magazine which blends business with sport and fashion'.

In each case the objective is stated broadly, as are the constraints. Right from the start, it should be noted, the brief includes a rough indication of the target market, the consumers for whom the project is being produced. This is an essential component of any brief. Almost never is a creative product targeted at the entire population, and with very good reason: almost no creative products can expect to be liked by 100 per cent of the population. Even massively successful creative products – like *Coronation Street*, or *The Sun*, or *Gone With the Wind* – never appeal to as many as half the population. The manager must therefore decide, as soon as possible and with as much precision as possible, the audience for whom the creative product is to be developed. The more exactly the audience can be defined, the more likely it is that the creatives will be able to come up with the perfect answer. Usually the definition of the target market can be tightened up and refined as the project proceeds. Here are some possible Stage II briefings, for the above projects:

'We need six 30-minute draft scripts for a situation comedy series based on a young hospital doctor and a young estate agent, sharing a flat in Fulham, with the plots built around their clashes of values . . . aimed primarily at unmarried ABC 16–34-year-olds living in the South-East . . .'

'Could you do eight floral fabric designs, simple bold colours, using only synthetics, that will retail at no more than £2 per metre . . . which will be for 35–59 year old housewives, C–Ds, in the Midlands and North, not very fashion conscious . . .'

'We're looking for a design recommendation for a monthly men's magazine to be called *Yep!* It'll run to about 112 pages, one-third editorial, two-thirds ads, 50/50 colour to black/white . . . aimed at a narrow target market of A class males, 18–29, unmarried, living in London or the smart suburbs, with high disposable income . . .'

The objectives, target markets and constraints have now been stated with greater precision, leaving the creatives with less freedom to flex their imaginations. At either stage, and with any brief, the creatives may wish to argue. The good manager will encourage and may even provoke such arguments, because they help the creatives to absorb and understand the brief more fully; this again is a point to which we will return shortly. If the creatives raise valid arguments, it is crucial for the manager to amend the brief, despite the fact that this usually means getting the revised brief approved by others in the organization who previously approved the original. Forcing creatives to work to a brief which both they and the manager know to be wrong – a not infrequent occurrence, absurd though it may sound – guarantees garbage.

None of which should be taken to imply that creatives abhor briefs, or the constraints within them. This is the way Barbara Nokes, Deputy Creative Director of the highly respected Bartle Bogle Hegarty advertising agency, puts it:[1]

'The creative process is generally preceded by sheer terror. You're confronted with a blank sheet of paper and a sharp pencil. You start with the brief, and the tighter the brief the easier it is to work to. If you know where the walls are you can travel down that narrow corridor and be completely wild. But if someone says it's an open brief you have no idea where to start.'

So briefs should always be as brief and as sharply focused as possible. Creatives, even more than the rest of us, get confused and discouraged if they have to wade through verbose and nebulous waffle. Managers who hope to give the creative imagination free rein by not mentioning constraints and limitations often believe, wrongly, that it is preferable for such constraints and limitations to be introduced into the project at a later stage, when it has more momentum.

Very occasionally, this approach succeeds; far more often it leads to imaginative ideas being mangled when they eventually collide with reality. The best creative managers do not hesitate to brief creatives fully, warts and all, from the start. The limitations and constraints are part of the challenge, to which the best creatives will respond with originality and vigour. Tim Bell explains:

'The best way to brief them is to narrow down the area in which you want them to be creative. Give them as many facts as you possibly can, answer as many questions as you possibly can, so that in the end their area of uncertainty is so tiny they can allow their imaginations to explode within it.

'Lead them in one direction, give them nowhere else to go. You should never go to them and say, "Have you got an idea about this product?" You must give them the selling idea, and then let them find a fantastically interesting and compelling way of expressing that idea.'

Sir Ralph Halpern agrees about the need for clear objectives:

'It is fundamental that the briefing gets across the objective of the work, to channel the creativity in the right direction, but without dictating the exact method by which it is to be done, which would stifle the creativity.'

And David Puttnam develops the point still further:

'The ultimate freedom for creative people is to allow them to work within specific and agreed bounds, bounds which they understand and appreciate. When I say understand, I mean they understand the reason for their existence. It's that thing about Pip in *Great Expectations* being told to go and play. You can't tell a child to "play". You can give him two sticks and say, "Would you like to go and play football with these?" and he'll say, "I can't". Or you can give him a patch of ground and a ball and see what he does with it. But you can't ask a child to "play". By the same token, I don't think you can just ask a creative person to create.'

Note David Puttnam's emphasis on agreement and understanding in the first two sentences. Some creative managers take a still more extreme view. Jeremy Isaacs views good briefings as an open discussion at the end of which a consensus agreement about the general direction to be taken will have been reached:

'If you want to explain to any group of people what some new project is likely to be, and to involve them, you have to explain it to them personally, you have to engage in a dialogue with them, you have to receive suggestions as to how the thing could develop before deciding how you want it to develop, and then implementing it.'

Jeremy Isaacs is here, of course, talking principally about Stage I briefings, as is Wally Olins who argues here that briefing is not a once-for-all event, but a continuous process of discussion and clarification which continues even while the work is progressing:

'The way in which you brief creative people is not at one meeting. It is a delusion to believe that you actually give a brief to somebody. It doesn't happen like that. What you do, in my experience, is over a period of days, weeks and even months, work together with the person who is designing the building or who is working on the identity programme, and you go through with them what it is that the client actually needs. The process of briefing is much more complex and more interactive than people believe. You get a great deal out of intense discussion over long periods about matters which don't appear to be germane, and only become germane when you see them in the context of the whole. Now that may be because the nature of my business is strategic and long-term.'

And at this stage neither he nor Isaacs is keen on the use of paperwork, which they believe to be anathema to creatives and to stifle creativity. Olins says:

'There's no point in writing memos, the creatives won't read them anyway. And if they do read them they will resent it because they will see it as a directive and they will see themselves being maligned and persecuted by a vast bureaucracy which is designed to crush their creative instinct.'

Isaacs makes much the same point:

'Creative people can't possibly respond to a bit of paper that reaches them saying, "What we want to do is XYZ". They can respond to a chat over a cup of coffee or a drink, in which you find out from them what it is they want to do . . . I think all management that is done by paper is bad management. Management, if it involves dealing with human beings, which is what I take it to mean, rather than simply ordering things, is a question of human relations, a question of working with people. You cannot do that on paper.'

Most managers, however, are anxious to commit things to paper quite quickly in the briefing process, at the very least to confirm in writing what has been agreed, as David Puttnam explains:

'Paper can be extremely useful if only to demonstrate to creative people the failure of their own logic. For example, if someone comes and sells me a project which is tremendously exciting but which has within it an area that worries me, I'll put that concern down on paper for them. It may be terribly valuable when you find out later that things haven't quite worked out. Creativity results from disciplined thinking. Paper helps you to create disciplined thinking in the artist.'

Tim Bell agrees:

'Briefs have to be written out, because otherwise everybody later disagrees about what was previously agreed. And memos are a bit more daunting than conversations. Perhaps my views are coloured because the copywriters I've worked with are impressed by the written word.'

Even Wally Olins and Jeremy Isaacs, despite their fear that paperwork will suffocate creativity, accept that written instructions are needed later in the creative process. Wally Olins makes the point especially clearly:

'The short-term and immediate matters with which we are concerned derive from a whole programme which has already been created, and for them you have to have a tight brief – if it's an eight-page folder or something like that. When you're producing something like a series of restaurants or a series of offices in a bank, and you have already done the strategic work, the technical work that you need to do falls into very tight parameters. And the briefing has got to be meticulous and accurately typed, and it has to deal with two things. In addition to the overall design strategy, it has to deal with time and money. No person in a creative business, as opposed to an artist, has any right to evade his responsibilities as far as time and money are concerned. If you evade your responsibilities for time and money you should not be in a business, you should be somewhere else.'

Time and money: the two thorns in the flesh of every creative manager. Adhering to time schedules and keeping to budgets are key management functions in any industry, but in the creative industries – for perfectly logical and understandable reasons, which we shall analyze in the next chapter – they are running sores, battles that must be perpetually fought yet can never be won. They are like evil gremlins inside every creative project, tinkering with the works, loosening the nuts and bolts so that at any moment it may career out of control.

In terms of the brief, it is always desirable for time and money constraints to be incorporated right from the start. No matter how vague, how insubstantial, how visionary the initial discussions, it will help if the manager outlines – if necessary in vague, visionary or insubstantial terms – the approximate financial scale of the project and an approximate timescale for its completion. As Barbara Nokes said, it helps the creatives as much as the manager. It provides them, from the beginning, with a framework within which to exercise their flights of fancy; it will provide them, from the beginning with a reminder that the project is commercial, not pure art; it provides them from the beginning, with realistic limits to sink their teeth into, and to dispute if they deem it necessary. To repeat David Puttnam's maxim, 'The ultimate freedom for creative people is to allow them to work within specific and agreed bounds, bounds which they understand and appreciate.'

Occasionally, creative managers, anxious to provoke creatives to levels of Utopian creativity way above and far beyond the ultimate freedom, say, 'Take as long as you like, money is no object'. They never mean it. (If they do, they should be fired.) They mean, but do not say: 'You're experienced creatives, so you have a pretty good idea of how much this kind of project would normally cost and how long it would normally take. On this occasion you can go completely over the top, because it is so important. And if you come up with the goods, somehow or other we'll find the time and money. Within reason, of course. We've worked together before, so I know I can rely on you, and you know you can trust me. We all know what's wanted, don't we?'

To prove that is what is meant, and that the creatives know perfectly well that is what is meant, it is only necessary to imagine the creatives returning to the manager with a real 'time and money no object' proposal. How about: 'In order to carry out this project properly we'll need to work on it for at least 30 years, and to do the work on planet Jupiter. Is that OK?' No, it would not be OK. However, 'time and money no object' can be, *to experienced creatives*, a reasonably clear if imprecise brief, which means, 'On this job you can exceed the norms by a fair margin in order to do something superlative'. The essential point being that it gives the creatives a rough notion of the time and money that could be made available. Completely neglecting to mention time and money does not achieve the same result at all. (This should not be taken to imply that 'time and money no object' is an admirable brief: it isn't. But used sparingly it can be an effective spur, and it is a good deal better than nothing.)

As a project moves on, and Stage II briefs come into existence, detailed time and money specifications become – as Wally Olins said – vital. Incidentally, the more accurately they can be specified right at the start, the less likely it will be that important executional stages will have to be rushed or carried out on a shoestring towards the project's end, because too much time and money have been frittered away earlier on.

In Stage II briefs the manager's attention to detail must be immaculate. No longer is the principle focus of his job the generation of soul-stirring creativity. The principal focus now must be accuracy, precision; getting the specification right in punctilious detail. As creative managers climb the ladder of success, they are able to concentrate to an increasing degree on Stage I briefs, which are the most fun, and to delegate Stage II briefs to sub-ordinates. However, such delegation can only be accomplished safely and successfully if the managers have the key items in the Stage II brief in the back of their minds. They will need to be aware of those items which could significantly affect timings and costs, and those items which could significantly affect the nature or quality of the end result. They will need the expertise to spot at a glance whether any of the specification details feels wrong, or could be symptoms of the evil gremlins at work. Few creative managers can get a feel for the rightness or wrongness of a specification unless they have produced such specifications themselves, when they were greenhorns.

This is an aspect of the creative manager's job that usually comes as a bit of a surprise to greenhorns. Less than amazingly perhaps, they expect the job to conform to its image: the thrills, spills and excitement of motivating creatives. They do not expect to find themselves arduously completing detailed briefing forms, full of boxes and sections that demand to be filled in with sizes, weights and measurements of all kinds, with timings and costings and legal requirements and approvals. But they quickly learn that if such briefing documents are completed incorrectly, all hell will break loose, and it may break loose from several directions at once. The creatives are furious because necessary information has not been supplied, or worse still has been supplied wrongly, so their work has been botched-up: the most heinous crime in their book. The senior creative managers are furious for all the obvious reasons, but most of all because the creatives are furious and they spend their lives trying to keep creatives calm and productive. The finance department is furious because money has been wasted; the customer or clients will be furious because their work has gone awry. And all because the briefing specification wasn't filled in properly.

Thus, it is all but impossible, as was said at the start of the chapter, to stress too strongly the importance of good briefing, at both Stages I and II. Briefs must inspire and intrigue yet at the same time constrain and control. They specify, as closely as can be specified, the 'amorphous something' that is required. But they cannot ensure that the evil gremlins are suppressed and that the specifications are carried out to the letter. How to do that is the subject of the next chapter.

Footnote

■

1. in *Campaign*, 9 June, 1989.

8

Time and Money

■

Benjamin Franklin's famous adage 'Time is money' might well have been coined for the creative industries – but for the fact that the creative industries hardly existed in Franklin's day. All industries own plant, hold stock, transform raw materials and suffer depreciation of capital, but in most of the creative industries the principal cost is human time. To quote another old adage often heard in creative businesses: 'The assets go down in the lift and home every night'.

The assets naturally incur certain overhead costs, in addition to their time. Congenial working conditions must be provided, as we've seen; they may need raw materials with which to exercise their creativity – and in the entertainments industries those raw materials can come expensive; creative products, like any others, must be marketed; and the creatives themselves need to be managed. Most of these overheads, though not all, vary in proportion to the creative time devoted to projects: more creative time means more overhead costs. Extra time means extra money. Every experienced financial controller in a creative organization knows that if the creative time spent on a project is reduced other overheads fall, as if by magic, and if creative time is increased other overheads grow, as if by magic. For this reason the economies of scale that can be achieved in the management of creativity are slight. The economies of scale that are to be found in the creative industries occur in distribution, manufacture (where this is relevant), financial systems and the purchase of other raw materials – but not in the purchase of the basic raw material, creativity.

So controlling the time spent is the first and fundamental key to controlling creative costs: time is of the essence.

It is perhaps important to state at this point that some creative managers feel that controlling time costs among creatives is not especially different from controlling them elsewhere. Look at what Paul Hamlyn, first, and then Michael Grade, have to say:

'Sure, timing is a problem, but it's also a problem with lawyers and accountants. You have certain people who do certain work for you, and you know they are very good, but they take their time. So you give them the sort of jobs where it doesn't matter if things slip, by a month or two. If you have a deadline you don't work with people who can't stick to deadlines.' (Hamlyn)

'I don't think keeping to time schedules is a function of being creative. Some creatives are very good at it, some are appalling. Similarly, some are very good at administration, some can't cope with it. But that's true of all executives. I don't see any distinction about creative people. Likewise, some creative people are very good at controlling costs, some aren't, some treat it like their own money, some don't.' (Grade)

Michael Grade, however, continues with an essential point:

'Administration, money, budgets . . . you can plug all these problems by giving the creative people support, so they can get on with being creative. You must never lose sight of the fact that what you are after is their creative flair.'

The problem, then, is not that all creatives are hopelessly and utterly incompetent. Certainly there is nothing in the creative personality, as we have analyzed it, that would suggest creatives are ordained by nature to be administratively inadequate. (Though it will be remembered that when they are working they tend to lose track of time.) The problem is not *all* creatives, at all. The problem is two-fold. First, some creatives who have exceptional talent happen to be administrative duffers. Second, the inherent nature of creativity – though not necessarily of creatives – makes it uniquely difficult to tie it down to time schedules.

With regard to the first, unarguably there are many creatives who cannot get their adrenalin pumping, who cannot get themselves into top gear, until they reach the deadline. This is not unique to creatives. It is a commonplace human trait. But it is especially

CREATIVE PEOPLE

prevalent, and extreme, among creatives. As Christopher Bland puts it:

'There are a lot of writers I know who admit that the truth is they never do anything until they're up against the deadline . . . "I don't start to get worried until it's Friday night and I'm going out to dinner and I know I've got to have it by nine o'clock the next morning" . . . Authors are always late. Always, always late.'

David Puttnam and Wally Olins, recognizing their own tendencies to procrastinate, are sympathetic to creatives' difficulties. Indeed, from his own description, Puttnam might well be one of Christopher Bland's errant authors:

'If I'm writing a piece for a newspaper I'll put it off and put it off and I'll persuade myself that I'm thinking about it, and that the longer I think the better it's going to be. The truth is you need the adrenalin to make you roll up your sleeves and sit down and do it. I often start at ten o'clock at night to do something for the following morning. I know it's wrong but. . .' (Puttnam)

'Writing books, I know that the deadline becomes an object I loathe and fear. In my mind, as I turn over the work, I decide it is impossible to meet the deadline, or if I do meet it I would be incapable of producing the best possible work. So within the creative mind you get this constant issue of the best being the enemy of the good. The creative man wants to make everything as good as he can, he doesn't mind if he sacrifices a month in order to improve it by three per cent. In other words, he loses his sense of proportion.' (Olins)

Having thus identified the problem, Olins goes on to postulate the way the manager should tackle it:

'The job of the manager is: (a) to enable the creative man to lose his sense of proportion where necessary, and (b) to remind him that he has to regain it if he wants to earn money at the end of the month. That is a very difficult balancing act. There are plenty of hacks who will produce rubbish on time and within cost constraints, and what we have to do as managers of highly creative people, is to enable the creative flame to exist in an atmosphere which is sympathetic. But they've got to understand that unless they operate within appropriate constraints of time and money, the company for whom they work will go broke. They have to understand that, and it's a very difficult thing for them to do.'

We'll return to the question of hacks in a moment, but this general approach to time management is widely accepted. Tim Bell says:

'I have a very simple view about it. We're not in art, we're in business, and there are deadlines. One of the reasons why creative people are paid large amounts of money is because they are supposed to understand commercial disciplines. That means, "Have an idea by Thursday". It may seem impractical, it may seem unfair, it may seem that you're likely not to get the best results – and all of those things may well be true – but the fact is that we are working in the world of commerce, and in the world of commerce there are deadlines that have to be met.'

Ralph Halpern and David Puttnam agree:

'The major problem in managing creative people is the control and monitoring of their work in progress. It has to be recognized that there is in general no logical approach to them achieving the work objective. Inspiration unfortunately does not conform to deadlines. However, deadlines must be met . . . The briefing for each creative will note each timing deadline and there will be agreed timing stages for completion of work to ensure these deadlines are met. There is, after all, no point in having the most beautiful range of Spring/Summer merchandise if it cannot be in the shops until Autumn.' (Halpern).

'Obviously in the making of a feature film timing is critical. Time really is money. So we are very precise in terms of the number of days, hours, minutes and seconds things are going to take. If they start to go too high, things are adjusted quickly – preferably before the actual filming starts.' (Puttnam)

That brings us to the first absolute rule about the control of time – and all other costs – on creative projects. It was implicit in Puttnam's earlier advice that creatives should always work within 'specific and agreed bounds, which they understand and appreciate'. The rule is: don't impose time schedules, agree them – in advance. The word 'negotiate' is almost more appropriate than the word 'agree', since there are frequently tussles between creatives and managers on the length of time any project will take. The creatives – seeking perfection – want more time; the managers – knowing time means money – want to give them less. However, as so often in the management of creativity, there are likely to be complex cross-currents in evidence: the creatives will want to finalize the work as quickly as possible, and win the expected acclaim, while the managers will want them to have as long as is reasonable to produce their best work. A good management rule of thumb is to get the creatives to state their ideal requirement, and then to lop off 20 per cent (one day in five). This will stretch the creatives without causing undue strain; and if the ten day job truly cannot be completed in eight days – a rare occurrence – the creatives can be relied upon to say so vehemently.

That, however, is an extra twist. The essential principle is the advance agreement, as Christopher Bland and David Puttnam point out:

'If the creative people are involved at the beginning, then there have to be exceptional circumstances for things to over-run. For the creative people it simply means going through the no doubt very tedious process of agreeing everything in advance, and working things out, and making sure they really think they can do it, and then sticking to what's been agreed.' (Bland)

'The system I use is consistent discipline, and supplying an optimum amount of information from the outset. I give the creative people *all* the information they can possibly want, so they can never say, "I didn't know that". They are partners, and since it is a genuine partnership you have got to share aims, and share problems.' (Puttnam)

Why then, despite everyone's best efforts, do creative projects so often over-run? Why are creatives so particularly prone to procrastinate?

'The time necessary for rehearsals,' aphorized Bertolt Brecht, 'is always one week longer than the time available.' Naturally, creatives share mankind's love of indolence. But as we have seen, their personalities push them towards being workaholic rather than idle. On the contrary, they tend to delay because being perfectionists, as Wally Olins said, the best is often the enemy of the good. They reject their own good ideas in an almost manic determination to do still better. It is not at all unknown for creatives to throw away marvellous work which they don't feel to be good enough, which others then rescue from their waste paper baskets late at night. That is not something which occurs in accountancy or personnel management.

The difficulty is accentuated because of the specific management problem, as David Puttnam put it earlier, that you are 'asking them to create something amorphous' – something which doesn't yet exist; something which by definition cannot yet exist, because if it does, creativity is not involved. The same is not true of, say, bottle manufacture or transport management. Production lines run at predictable speeds, journeys take a fairly predictable time. Nothing much changes from week to week or month to month, so the managers can know exactly how long things will take; and when things do change, the consequences of the change are usually calculable. Creativity isn't like that. Every project is a new project. Experienced players can estimate roughly how long things will take, and tough managers will ensure they take no longer; but that does not mean that the timing of creative work can be equated with the timing of bottle production. (That is why hacks, to pick up Olins' earlier point, find no difficulty in delivering on time: they produce their work to rote, without being creative).

At first sight it might seem strange, as Tim Bell said, to demand of anyone that they should have a great, original idea, for a fabric design, or a television programme, or an advertisement, by next Thursday. But that is the nature of the industries in which creatives work. Successful creatives must be able to originate good ideas to order; and the more fecund the creative, the faster he will be able to do so. Many of the world's greatest artists have produced masterpieces at an astonishing rate of knots. In addition to Mozart, Shakespeare was no slouch; and Balzac and Dickens turned out their serialized novels to unforgiving monthly deadlines. So it can be done, even at the highest levels of creativity. Nonetheless, the manager who constantly suspects that creatives who are not overtly creating must be idling is more likely to stimulate paranoia than outstanding original work. The great novelist, William Thackeray, for example, described himself 'sitting for hours before my paper, not doing my book but incapable of doing anything else'.[1]

'Inspiration,' as Sir Ralph Halpern said, 'unfortunately does not conform to deadlines.' And managers should never underestimate the neurotic niggling that nags ever more obsessively in the creative mind as the deadline approaches and the great idea has not yet been conjured up.

One effective way to constrain time costs is to control the costs, instead of (or rather as well as) controlling the time. In other words, to employ cheaper creatives. As was emphasized in Chapter 1, the remuneration of creatives closely reflects the demand for their services. So if creatives' time can be bought cheaply it means either: (a) that they are young, inexperienced, and still learning, or (b) that the marketplace does not value their talents highly, or (c) that they are especially keen, for some reason, to take on the job.

The employment of young and inexperienced creatives carries obvious risks, and equally obvious potential benefits. Naturally, the greatest caution must be applied to projects which are especially time-sensitive, or where sizeable expenditure is involved. As long as there is time for the job to be re-done if necessary, without the loss of too much money, it makes excellent sense to employ apprentices, who may bring completely new thinking and a refreshing approach to the project. From the manager's point of view, the risk will be further contained if he can ensure that the young tyros are constantly and closely supervised by superiors able – and perhaps more importantly, willing – to spend the necessary time. In advertising and fashion particularly, much excellent creativity stems from youngsters who are employed, at almost deplorably low salaries, by companies which specialize in training them, encouraging them – and then losing them.

There are also times when it makes sense to employ inexpensive creatives whose talents the marketplace does not value highly. (If this were not the case they would never be in work; or more accurately, they would only ever get work from inept managers.) As was pointed out in Chapter 4, it is the creative manager's responsibility to decide upon the level of quality necessary, justifiable, and affordable, for every job. In some creative businesses there may be specialist buyers, with the necessary experience to be able to be of assistance. However, general buying departments, which may be marvellously skilled at negotiating bargain prices for computers and toilet rolls, should be avoided at all costs. It should hardly need to be stressed, at this stage in the book, that buying creativity is not like buying computers and toilet rolls. That is not to say that creative suppliers cannot be bargained down. On the contrary, they can, and almost always should be. But because creativity is so nebulous, and specifying creative quality is all but impossible, buying it is a specialist task. Indeed, in the United States a new breed of freelance creative buyer, or 'cost consultant', is springing up in many creative industries to help restrain the soaring costs of creativity.[2]

Creatives, as has been said, are sometimes willing to accept lower salaries or fees to work – either full-time or on a freelance basis – with companies or on jobs which especially appeal to them. This is, once again, something which occurs in all walks of life but is of particular consequence in the creative industries. Creatives will accept less to work for 'fashionable' organizations; or to work in organizations where they can expect to improve and sharpen their talent; or to work on projects with high creative prestige, which may win them public plaudits and creative awards.

Employing talented creatives at bargain rates obviously has its financial attractions. Managers must be wary, however. Creatives can be expected to be even more than usually egotistical if they have chosen to work at a discount, or below market rates, in order to achieve personal prestige and acclaim.

The question at the heart of most creative cost problems is: what is the value of perfection? 'There is hardly anything in the world,' aphorized the great critic and social reformer, John Ruskin, 'that some man can't make a little worse and sell a little cheaper.' And in the creative industries the converse is also true: there is hardly anything in the world that some creative can't make a little better, but it will cost a great deal more. As Ruskin implied, defining the price, and value, of quality is a universal problem, and always has been. In most industries, however, it is possible to calculate with considerable accuracy the cost-effects of quality improvements, or impairments; and to make at least an approximate estimate of the likely effect upon consumer demand. Modern market research techniques can now help companies make such estimates with a fair degree of precision. Computer analyses can help companies investigate the probable results of a wide variety of adjustments to costs, margins and prices, no matter how complex the inter-relationships between the various factors involved. With the exception of personnel decisions, few if any major business decisions are made today which do not involve the study of computerized predictions of the possible consequences. A very large number of business decisions can be reduced to mathematical analysis, and though the computer cannot make the decisions, it is an invaluable guide – particularly in the area of cost control.

Almost none of this, however, applies to creativity. No computer can, or ever will, be programmed to tell you whether one design is better than another, whether one orchestration will be more popular than another, whether one actress is better in the part than another. No computer can, or ever will, be programmed to tell you whether two subtle colours harmonize or clash, whether one copywriter's adjective will be more telling than another, whether one type of brick matches another or does not. At certain stages in every creative project, market research can be employed – if the size of the project will bear it – and may provide rough guidelines, as we shall see. Of course computers are used throughout the creative industries, to handle and process all sorts of data. But the infinite majority of tiny decisions that have to be made on every creative project – size of typeface, shade of blue, timbre of sound, use of punctuation, etc. – are, must be, and forever will be, taken subjectively and quickly. This is a crucial point about creativity which differentiates it from all other industrial activities.

From the manager's point-of-view, he must rely continually on the creatives' judgment. It is the creatives' role to make all the minuscule decisions which in total constitute the entire project. Their success will depend on their ability to make such decisions correctly. The great majority of the decisions – size of typeface, shade of blue, timbre of sound, use of punctuation – have no cost implications. But others do, and if the cost implications are of significance, the manager must know, and be involved in the decision.

As with time schedules, the absolute rule about all costs is that they need to be agreed in advance. And as with time schedules, there are often complex cross-currents at work, as Jeremy Isaacs here points out:

'You have to have gone through the budget with several tooth combs from the word go, and to have satisfied yourself that the project can be made within budget. That often means increasing the budget so that at least you know you have made a realistic commitment . . . "We are kidding ourselves if we think we can get it done for that, it will end up twice over budget. So if we want to do it we are going to have to resign ourselves, from the word go, to the fact that that is what it is going to cost". Creative people sometimes resist that – they say, "No, no, you must be joking, it won't cost anything like that, I wouldn't dream of asking you for all that much". They are worried that if it is going to cost that much the manager's going to say, "No, we can't afford to do it". And that may sometimes happen. But anyway it's essential first to get the budget right, and that has to be built on realistic assumptions.

'I think that the fatal and dreadful and irresponsible thing for the creator to do is, either by secrecy, or by tunnel vision or by megalomania, to drive a coach and horses through financial barriers. That is a disgraceful thing to do and should never be tolerated by any organization.'

Christopher Bland wholeheartedly agrees about the importance of involving creatives early in budgeting planning:

'Television cost-consciousness has grown very considerably in the last two or three years. Programme budgets used to be regarded as guesses, not things to be adhered to or to be taken too seriously. Now programme budgets are looked at very hard and they are looked at by the creative people, too. Budgets used to be something the accountants did, and the creative people thought: "We'll make the programme and they'll tell us whether we overspent or underspent". It would rarely be the latter. Now there is more creative involvement in the active planning of budgets.'

However, the initial problem, as Isaacs implies (and returning to John Ruskin), is how to set the original budget, given that the best will cost more, and no computer will be able to give you even an inkling of whether or not it will be worth it. Like the spotting and selection of talent, these decisions will always be judgmental, made on the basis of instinct, hunch and experience. That does not mean that they should be either random or illogical. The crucial issue the manager must perpetually keep in mind is the *total* cost budget, whether the items under consideration can be met within it and, most important of all, whether the eventual income – be it sales revenue, fees or whatever – will fully cover that cost. This is how David Puttnam perceives the problem:

'The game I play as a manager is: can we tell the story in such a way as it will interest and reach a large audience – in which case it justifies large resources. Or are we going to attempt something which maybe has its own integrity, but which is likely to reach only a small audience and so justifies only a small budget. A most interesting case in point was *The Killing Fields*. Despite its subject matter, we decided to aim the film at the optimum potential audience. We acknowledged and took on board certain compromises. And we made the film accordingly. It was a successful decision. We made the same assessment on *The Mission*. But we didn't carry it through. We never really solved the problems of the film in its first 25 minutes, and the film never recovered from that. You've got to be honest with yourself when you are asking for resources. You've got to be able to say to yourself: with a fair wind and with a decent bit of luck, you will be able to recover, recoup and repay those resources. That's the job of the manager, and sometimes you go wrong.'

This is not that different to Sir Ralph Halpern's approach, in the world of fashion:

'In the area of clothes design, commercial reality dictates the value of a garment. There is no point in producing a beautiful dress which costs £99 if the customer is only prepared to pay £9.99. Costs are controlled by ensuring that the brief for the design includes the commercial value of the dress.'

Nor is Jeremy Isaacs' approach too dissimilar, though from a some-what different perspective:

'First of all, you have to operate within your own budget. You have to operate within your own resources. If you don't operate within your own resources as a manager of a creative institution you will bankrupt the institution and put yourself out of a job. You then roughly apportion those resources between the differ-ent projects that you know you have in the schedule in a particu-lar year – one or two of them you may allow, within the available budget, to approach as near perfection as possible. You decide to back this one all the way. That is a purely subjective judgment: I'm going to back these people all the way. Other people I'm going to ask to work within sterner financial constraints.

'If you back people all the way and they deliver something that is both creatively unsuccessful and also commercially unsuccessful, you've made a very bad judgment indeed, and if that is your track record you're not going to be a very successful manager. If you make such a judgment and the thing is creatively successful and commercially unsuccessful, well at least you've got something you can point to with pride. If you're hugely fortunate and come up with something that is both creatively successful and commercially successful then you get medals. But those are very difficult managerial decisions, and I have to say that luck must play a certain part. The important thing is never to allow the down side, the risk of any potential decision going wrong, to be so all pervasive as to destroy what you are trying to do.'

All of these analyses reflect the manager's Janus-like role. He is aiming to balance the creatives' ambitions with the requirements, and the potential, of the marketplace. The manager's overall strategy – the desired outcome – will define the total resources that can be afforded, the total costs that can be justified. It is within the total that the tiny decisions will be judgmental, as David Puttnam relates:

'You have to make judgments. You have to assess whether you are dealing with something that's truly important, or just something that's ego-based and whimsical. Visconti on his sets would put very, very expensive china in the cupboards even if nobody ever opened the cupboards. He believed it enhanced the way the actors performed on set. He once purchased 12 silk shirts to go into a drawer, which would never be seen – so that Burt Lancaster, playing his role, would feel his hand slide between the silk shirts when he went to the drawer to pull out a purse.'

Patently, Visconti's producers had decided, in Isaac's phrase, 'to back him all the way'. Equally, knowing Visconti's style, they doubtless built the cost of his little extravagances into the original budget, if they were doing their job correctly.

Once the schedule has been agreed, and the costs have been agreed, how, finally, does the manager ensure that the creatives do not, Cimino-like, drive a coach and horses through the barriers? This is an issue in which the cost-per-project is inextricably bound-up; and so, not infrequently, are lawyers.

Low-cost projects obviously do not merit intricate cost and time controls. The cost of the controls might easily exceed the cost of the project. The manager must trust the creative to operate within the constraints agreed, and establish through experience – as Paul Hamlyn explained – which creatives require latitude and which do not. The smallness of the job in no way abrogates the necessity for prior agreement about timing and costs – almost the reverse, since once the items have been agreed the manager may well expect to pay no further attention to them until the project is completed. If he then meets any unpleasant surprises he must make his displeasure known, forcibly. The nature of low-cost creative projects inherently means, as has been pointed out, that there will be lots of them. The manager must adapt his style accordingly. Precedent and consistency are all-important. So are continuing relationships, as manager and creatives move from job to job, each learning the other's weaknesses and strengths. It is perhaps because Paul Hamlyn and Michael Grade have learned to do all this instinctively that they feel, as they said at the beginning of this chapter, that controlling creatives is not that different from controlling other people.

High-cost projects must be handled quite differently. All those managers involved in high-cost projects agree it to be essential to appoint supervisors – whatever their title, which varies for industry to industry – to keep a close and watchful eye on the creatives' progress. Here are three clear statements of principle:

- 'You can't expect creatives to administrate their own expenditure. You've got to give them really competent people to monitor what they're spending. Preferably production people, because then the creatives feel they're sympathetic, rather than accountancy people who they think are the enemy.' (Tim Bell)

- 'You need systems of financial control whereby certain expenditures can only be authorized by the positive act of a responsible manager, and where all expenditures against budget are reported to a central financial control system at the very least weekly and ideally daily. Then when things begin to go wrong – like we've only got a quarter of the footage shot for this movie and we've spent half the budget – you get some advance warning and you can move in to try and get control.' (Jeremy Isaacs)

- 'To control costs you must put a really tough accountant on the production, who won't let them overspend, and who will control things all the time. Because if he doesn't you'll get an over-run. Even if he does you may get an over-run because he can't control every aspect of the process.

'He will monitor costs on a daily basis, but what he can't monitor is the value of what's in the can, relative to producing the whole thing. He will know X amount of footage has been shot, and Y is the budget, and he's got Z left to play with. What he can't know, is when the director will say: "I can't use that . . ." after it's already been shot. He just can't monitor that. Nobody can.

'If you're making a series you should know within the first week if you're over-spending. If it takes two or three programmes, two or three episodes to discover, then you're in real trouble, somebody's cocked it up. It isn't necessary. You ought to be able to discover weekly. It's not difficult. You may choose to ignore it, that's your prerogative. But if it takes two or three programmes then you've got very bad control systems.' (Christopher Bland)

This is something Jeremy Isaacs confirms from his personal experience – an example, to reiterate his earlier point, of the advantages of having worked on both sides of the fence:

'I always tried to work within budgets and quite often in my life have had to work within very severe time constraints. I mean you just have to finish by a certain date because the programme is going out every week. I found that the single most difficult thing to do. When I knew I had something that wasn't good enough and that a really creative fellow wouldn't have done, I nevertheless knew it had to be broadcast Thursday. Halfway through the *World at War*, it turned out it was going to cost in the end twice what I'd estimated it would cost.

'But I wouldn't have fired myself for that. Because of the reporting of costs system, I was able to take my employers along with me. And it was already apparent, when two of the programmes were finished out of 23, that other companies were beginning to be interested in buying them, and that Thames Television was going to make a great deal of money out of the series. Therefore, they could perfectly rationally decide: it now looks as if it's going to cost £2X rather than £X, but we can see that what we're getting is something that we very much want.'

Isaacs was perhaps lucky because *World at War* was, deservedly, a phenomenal success. That is by no means always the case when budgets are overspent. The making of *Heaven's Gate* is a sublime example of creatives disregarding agreed schedules. The director over-ran at every single stage: after 12 days shooting the picture was ten days behind. The film was initially scheduled to take 69 shooting days. It finally opened about two years late. This is Steven Bach's description of how such calamities occur:

'It is not unusual – it may even be routine – for a picture to experience difficulties in the early days of shooting, particularly when the work is on location. If the picture is a big one and the conditions are in any way primitive, these problems can grow geometrically or exponentially . . . Every picture is different from every other picture and has its own unknowns, its own problems, requiring solutions often unique, often without precedent for those who are expected to deliver considerable ingenuity on critically short notice . . . Accordingly, if experience in the movie business teaches anything, it is that it doesn't teach *everything*'.

As was mentioned previously, United Artists, who were backing *Heaven's Gate*, felt themselves in a weak position *vis-à-vis* the director, Michael Cimino, because they desperately wanted his then glittering creative reputation to bolster their tarnished one; and as Puttnam has stressed, when creatives gain the whip hand over management, disaster is likely to ensue. *Heaven's Gate* became a *cause célèbre* precisely because everything about it was so outrageous. Fortunately, few creative projects go off the rails so wildly. In part at least, that is because managers have developed the scheduling techniques necessary to control them. Wally Olins summarizes cost-control problems thus:

'It's up to the management of the organization to manage the business properly. When you get to a phase where you're doing a job and the creative people say, "We're worried we're going to go over budget because we need to produce something but we haven't got enough money", and the client says we can't have any more money, I may well say we will take a loss on the job because we have to do it right because that's the ethos of the company. The good manager of creative people has to judge where to go on and on, and if necessary go way over budget. And if you get it back you get it back, and if you don't you don't. Sometimes it's worth it, and sometimes it is simply a bloody waste of time, self-indulgent rubbish.'

Extra costs can creep in even after a project is nominally finished. Note, for example, this memo about the film *Funny Girl*, written by Alan Hirschfield, then President of Columbia Pictures: 'Now that this picture is completed the most difficult job all of us have is holding down additional expense. It appears to me that the cost could rise substantially if the producer is allowed to have free rein of continuing expenditure. At some point someone is going to have to say no to some of the requests or all of the very good efforts that were made to hold down costs during production will be overshadowed by the post-production expenditures. I believe it is very important that a very hard line be taken in this regard.'[3] As Hirschfield stressed, to overspend previously agreed and determined budgets is generally unacceptable, and those managers who allow it to occur too often soon find themselves out of work.

Why are creative budgets so frequently overspent? The problem goes to the heart of the management of creativity. Because the end-product is 'amorphous' before it is started, the possibility must always exist that it could be improved while in progress. Improved commercially that is, not just aesthetically to please the creatives. If the manager keeps a tight clamp on the costs he risks diminishing the commercial potential of the work. Despite which the basic rule must stand: costs must be clamped. On the other hand, as everyone knows, rules are made to be broken – very, very, occasionally.

There is, however, one area of cost control where the rules must never be broken: the control of rip-offs. There is no data to prove the point, and there probably never will be, but it seems certain that rip-offs – particularly bribery and expense-account fiddles – are more prevalent in certain of the creative industries than in any other fields. In the record business corruption was rampant in the past, but appears to be less common now. In the movie business cheating is still widespread:[4]

'According to knowledgeable people in the film industry, bribes, payoffs, and other financial improprieties almost certainly run into millions of dollars annually. The dealings are said to take a variety of forms, and include the following:

'Bribes paid by independent motion-picture and television producers to studio executives who are in a position to approve a project . . . Bribes paid by independent television producers – after a network pilot is made – to members of network programming departments whose influence is important in winning approval of a proposed television series . . . Loans made to studio executives . . . by independent producers or agents who, because of the debt, can virtually call the shots in negotiating a high-cost deal. The deal contains extra money that, in effect, is stolen from the company . . . Bribes to film company executives from theatre owners who want favourable treatment or play time on a new film . . . Besides these practices, industry sources say there are other forms of corruption [ranging from] payoffs by production companies to union officials for favourable arrangements on a movie project, to expenditures of large amounts of company funds to underwrite personal living expenses.'

All of which is often euphemistically called 'creative accounting'. It is not an aspect of creativity with which the wise manager will want to have much truck.

Finally, a visiting Martian might ask, why can't all these intractible difficulties be resolved by lawyers, with well drawn-up contracts that will ensure things are completed on time, without rip-offs and within budget, and that ferocious penalties will be exactable if they are not? That, after all, is how things are done in other industries. Well as has already been stated, the creative industries do spawn more than their fair share of contracts, and contracts sometimes help; but they are rarely a complete answer.

First, there is the 'amorphous' problem – courts find it hard to decide whether or not creativity has been completed to specification. Second, contracts are much more effective as a means of stopping people doing things than as a means of forcing them to do things – particularly when it comes to forcing them to have ideas. Third, many if not most creative jobs happen far too quickly for there to be time to get lawyers and contracts involved. Fourth, the costs-per-project are frequently far too small to warrant the involvement of lawyers and contracts. Fifth, legal processes are so slow that it can be months, and often years, before judgment is given – and still more costs are then incurred. Sixth, exacting financial penalties from individuals is hideously difficult – if the creatives didn't pay, would they be imprisoned? Seventh, which creatives would want to work for organizations that might incarcerate them?

Even the best design control systems in the end come down to personal relationships and personal involvement, as Jeremy Isaacs explains:

'You just have to keep saying, "We've only got three more weeks left, Bill, we've only got two more weeks left, we've only got one more week left, three more days left, and we can't go on for a week longer because the money for that extra week isn't there". It's endless chivying to get finished on time.'

Happily the problems are not quite so overwhelming as any chapter which concentrates upon them must inevitably make them sound. For as Wally Olins neatly puts it:

'There is a spectrum. There are a number of highly creative, highly imaginative people who are self-disciplined, who manage themselves extremely well – and are therefore extremely easy to manage.'

Footnotes

∎

1. in Harding, R. E. M. (1940) *An Anatomy of Inspiration*, Cambridge: W. Heffer.
2. 'Cost consultants are members of a fast-growing fraternity with a single mission: to help advertisers control the escalating price of producing television commercials', in Robins, M. J. (1989) 'Windsong Was on His Mind', *The New York Times Magazine*, 2 April.
3. in McClintick, D. (1982) *Op. cit*.
4. *The New York Times*, 16 January, 1978.

9

Yes, No, or Maybe

∎

At last the creatives have settled down to work: sketching, scribbling, typing, gazing unseeingly into the distance, struggling to nudge their personal muse into life with every wile and ruse at their disposal. They know (or think they know) what is required, who the target is, how long they've got, how much they can spend, and all the constraints within which they must work. Should they be left alone? Or should the manager drop in on them now and again to see how things are going?

There is no universal answer. It depends on the creative, not on the manager. The standard management textbook advice is that the manager should not try to get involved too soon:

> 'Nothing will inhibit the creative process more than being critical of an idea when it first emerges. This does not mean that criticism, judgment and evaluation have no place in the generation of new ideas. But they should come into play only at the conclusion of the creative process.'[1]

One of America's foremost management gurus, Professor Peter F. Drucker, supports this view unequivocally:

> 'The best thing you can do for creative people is just get out of their way. Give them a task and leave them alone.'[2]

Unarguably there are talented creatives who resent, and cannot cope with, having to explain ideas which are still in gestation. Sometimes this is plain cussedness, but sometimes it is an unavoidable consequence of the way they work. Typists and bricklayers generally start jobs at the beginning and work through to the end, but many creatives proceed haphazardly, as new thoughts come to them. There are excellent scriptwriters who habitually work back from a punch-line, and still succeed in creating a convincing story. P. G. Wode-house wrote his chapters in higgledy-piggledy order and blended them together as the book took shape; John Cleese has described how he and Connie Booth wrote each of the *Faulty Towers* episodes, constructing the plots on huge sheets of paper, and reorganizing them again and again; prize-winning novelist John Irving starts by figuring out the end of the book, then works backwards, beginning each chapter from the rear as well; we have already seen how Mozart would build a whole symphony in his head, before committing it to paper. None of them, it may be assumed, would have responded warmly to zealous managers asking them to 'show me how things are getting on'. They could be expected to endorse, as would many creatives, Professor Drucker's advice.

Not all creatives seek such solitude, however. Some need constant reassurance, and like to show people their work frequently during its development. Naturally they prefer to show their work to those whose opinions they respect. Nor do they always accept the opinions they receive. Lots of excellent creatives continually 'test the water'. They invite criticism, listen, consider it thoughtfully, and then reject 99 per cent of it. This may be frustrating for the critic, but can be exceedingly beneficial to the creative, as it helps him to perceive his work through others' eyes, and to probe its strengths and weaknesses.

The varying ways in which creatives work may reflect basic differences in their psychologies, as Dr. Anthony Storr spotlights:[3]

'Great artists who are predominantly of depressive temperament may, like Michelangelo, produce masterpieces over which they have had to labour for years. The less gifted, or the more deprived, may not be able to tolerate long intervals between obtaining the supplies of self-esteem which they need. Some writers, for example, are so driven to produce short works in rapid succession that they never do themselves justice. The immediate rewards of journalism are seductive in this respect. Seeing oneself in print every week, or even every day, is immensely reassuring to some characters. But this need for recognition carries the disadvantage that it may preclude the production of more serious, lengthy work. Many journalists cannot face the long period without reward demanded by writing a novel. They "want it now"; and having found a way of getting it cannot give up this source of immediate satisfaction.'

Creatives working within a large organization can, to some degree at least, get the best of both worlds – if their psychology so demands. They can take the time necessary (or anyway the time permitted) to do the job to the best of their ability, and seek regular 'supplies of self-esteem' in the process. Supplying these doses of self-esteem is part of the manager's job, and most managers welcome it because it allows them to keep an eye on the work as it progresses, and to reassure themselves that it's on the right lines.

Creatives who prefer to labour alone, like hermits, and emerge from their seclusion with the creative work parcelled-up and finalized, give the managers sleepless nights and nervous breakdowns. However, as Dr Storr implies, the differing working methods of different creatives are embedded deep in their psychology. So managers who try to force the hermits to keep presenting their work before they are ready – or conversely, managers who refuse to look at work which is incomplete, even if the creative asks them to – will soon find those particular creatives unwilling and unable to work with them. Creatives do not come in uniform psychological shapes and sizes. The manager must be sufficiently flexible (and flexible does not mean weak) to adapt his style in order to help them optimize their output.

If he has sufficient power and authority, however, the manager can take a conscious and explicit decision not to work with particular types of creatives, or with creatives who work in particular ways. Inevitably, this will preclude him from working with certain individuals, some of them perhaps highly talented, who are unable to work in the way required. Wally Olins has made exactly this kind of decision. The way his company operates demands that creatives work openly and that the fruits of their labour are available to continual inspection. It will be remembered from Chapter 6 that his building has been designed specifically to facilitate such openness. ('We don't want a situation emerging where people are secretly working for days or weeks, nights or weekends . . .') This is one of the company's basic precepts:

'That is the way the company has always worked, from the very beginning. Anyone who comes into this company is not told those are the rules, they see those are the rules. And whatever they learnt before they have to forget. Because peer group pressures here are so great. There are teams of people, and these teams keep on inspecting one another.'

Without question, Olins' system offers considerable advantages, particularly with regard to the amendment and rejection of work, which we will be considering further in a moment. However, there are also disadvantages, as he himself admits:

'The teams keep changing. Everybody works in the open. If somebody's a bastard then everybody knows he's a bastard, and everybody says he's a bastard, and they say, "Do I have to work with that bastard?" . . . Sometimes it isn't worth paying a high emotional price for talent, and you have to get rid of them.'

Were Olins willing, or able, to allow the 'bastard' to hide away somewhere, in a cubby-hole, he might conjure up ideas which, in William Wordsworth's famous lines, 'flash upon that inward eye which is the bliss of solitude';[4] he might contribute immense creativity to Olins' organization, without antagonizing and alienating members of a team. However, the employment of such loners would not be compatible with Olins' approach to briefing, and perhaps even more importantly, would raise other management problems which Olins' system successfully solves.

It is often said that creatives 'take criticism badly'. That is generally true, though few people in any walk of life take criticism well. It is one of humanity's little foibles. With creatives, however, the inability to take criticism is especially apparent, because they are continuously 'being judged by their output'; and as we have seen, they view their output as an extension of themselves, as a reflection of their character and their ego. So when the manager criticizes one of their creations, he is not criticizing some abstract artefact, but them. This is clearly recognized by most creative managers. Jeremy Isaacs, for example, explains it thus:

'It's only natural they should take rejection harder because they put so much of themselves into what they are doing. They do not put their work forward in a routine sort of way, they put it forward in a very serious kind of way. So you have to be very, very certain that when you propose a change to somebody you have very, very good reasons for it.'

Christopher Bland's views are similar:

> 'You have to do it and recognize that it is painful. But it's a
> highly subjective and therefore rather bruising process. It always
> boils down to "I don't think it's good," or "I don't think it's good
> enough," or "I don't think it's any good at all". However you
> dress it up, however good your creative credentials, it is very
> painful for the guy on the receiving end. That's true whether
> it's a piece of copy, or a manuscript for a novel or a piece of
> film, whether it's documentary or drama. You have to tell them.
> Telling them *why* is hard. You can't say, as you can with the
> iron foundry casting, look it's the wrong size, or it's got holes in
> it. With creative work it's a subjective judgment. You have to
> say, "That doesn't work," "It doesn't look right," or "It doesn't
> hold together". Try telling an actress that her voice isn't right,
> that she's not performing well. It's very bruising.'

Nonetheless it must be done. The importance of rejecting unsatisfactory work has already been stressed. From the creatives' point of
view the manager must act as leader, controller, critic and demander
of excellence. What has not been stressed is the importance of quality
control from the customers' point of view. The manager, as has
repeatedly been stressed, is the interface between the creatives and
other people, and it is to them that he will have to answer if the
creative work is unsatisfactory. Often the manager will need to persuade them that the work is right – sell it to them, either personally
or indirectly. The marketing of creativity is a subject to which we'll
return in the next chapter.

But however good a salesman the manager is, and however glib
his tongue, he should never attempt to sell creative work knowing
it to be wrong and knowing it could be improved. Sometimes things
aren't that clear. Sometimes the manager will have an uneasy feeling
about the work, a feeling that it isn't quite right, that maybe it could
be better – but will be unable quite to pinpoint why or how. On
such occasions he must rely on the creatives' judgment, and must
present their work to colleagues and customers with as much confidence as can be mustered. Such uncertainties are inherent in the
nature of creativity. As has already been said, there are no creative
products about which absolutely everyone agrees. All of us see films,
watch TV shows, hear records and gaze at fashions about which we
are unable to make up our minds. However, the manager is not paid

to be indecisive. So if he cannot make up his own mind, he must rely on the creatives.

In any case, such indecisiveness should be rare. If the manager is capable of doing the job, he must be able to decide, quickly, whether the creative work meets the brief. Note the phrase 'meets the brief', since this is a frequent source of contention between creatives and managers. In an ideal world – or so creatives would have it – managers would take responsibility only for the 'content' of creative work (the brief), while the creatives themselves would be responsible for its 'form', or style. In other words, to return to the imaginary briefs in Chapter 6, the managers would decide whether or not the creative work in each case met the required specifications: the creatives would decide whether the TV serial was amusing, whether the fabric designs were attractive, whether the magazine design was sophisticated. 'Aesthetic' decisions, the creatives argue, are outside of the competence of the manager, and so must be the prerogative of those with the necessary talent to make sensitive judgments – other, more senior, writers and designers perhaps; but not managers.

To some degree, most managers accept this point of view. On the other hand, the manager knows that his customers and colleagues will not be too bothered about the metaphysical dividing lines that creatives draw between content and form. If those concerned do not like, and won't accept, the humour of the TV series, or the designs of the fabric, or the style of the magazine, they will not be mollified by being told that the brief was carried out correctly in all other respects. Hence the manager is forced to become involved in the aesthetics of creative projects. The extent to which he feels the need to do so will depend, in great measure, upon the trust and confidence the manager places in the creatives working on the project. This boundary between form and content in creative work, between creative and managerial responsibility, is, and forever will be, a verbal battleground. As long as both sides are evenly matched, the importance of which has already been frequently emphasized, the outcome will be superior creative work.

Here Michael Grade describes encounters which all managers of creativity know well:

'It's difficult to argue logically about whether or not colours are right, and it's just as difficult to argue about characters on a page. It's all subjective. It's all, in the end, about choices and tastes. Every kind of creative decision is about choices and tastes. So those subjective arguments occur with all kinds of creative people.'

If the manager is asking the creative to alter a piece of work, rather than to start again, it means the manager has found a kernel in the work which he suspects could be turned into something much better: he is saying 'maybe'. The good creative manager will deliberately foster the ability to spot gems buried in irrelevant or misdirected debris. More important still, he will be able to redirect the creative's enthusiasm, so that the gem will be polished to achieve its maximum effect – not thrown away, often by its creator, in a welter of temperamental dissension. Sir Ralph Halpern seeks always to turn rejection into amendment, by convincing the creatives that they themselves want to carry out the changes:

'Creative people's ability to produce is based entirely on their self-confidence. To reject their ideas is to erode that confidence. Instead, the creatives must be skilfully manipulated to believe it is they who wish to reject or amend their own work. It is their idea to change the work.'

Professor William G. Kirkwood, of East Tennessee State University, in a paragraph headed, 'Learn to Build On Ideas As Well As Criticize Them', puts the point thus:[5]

'Remember to actively look for the strengths in any idea you or others develop. As weaknesses become apparent, don't dismiss a concept altogether; seek ways to correct its flaws while retaining its strong points. This can be done using a three-step process.

'When you wish to respond to an idea, first note its strengths. True, the idea might not be right in its present form, but are any parts of the concept useful? Are the goals of the idea positive, even if more work is needed to achieve them? Does the philosophy that inspired the idea seem to be on the right track? Only after you've identified the concept's strengths should you address its shortcomings. Last, for each weakness you see, develop a means to overcome the flaw while preserving positive features.'

That final piece of advice is one about which many creative managers would have misgivings. All would agree that it is desirable to look for strengths and positive features, before looking for weaknesses and shortcomings. But, in Britain at least, most creative managers prefer to hand the job back to the creatives for amendment, rather than try to improve it themselves, or even jointly with the creatives. As Jeremy Isaacs says:

'If you're inclined to re-do it yourself, you're in desperate trouble.'

That, however, does not contradict the essential requirement to provide criticisms, which are as detailed as possible, as Tim Bell explains:

'As far as amendment is concerned, my technique is to confront it with detailed comments: "Isn't there a better piece of music?", or "Couldn't we cast somebody better?" or "The dialogue's not very tight," or "That third line doesn't add an awful lot" '.

That is the manager espousing his correct role, setting the problem, the challenge – not demotivating the creatives by offering (probably uncreative) solutions of his own.

If the work cannot be usefully amended, is beyond salvation, the manager must bite the bullet and throw it out. Rejection involves three common difficulties. First, too much time has already been invested for it to be possible to start again. Second, too much money has already been invested, and the waste would be unaffordable. Third, too much of the creative's ego has already been invested, and to start again would be hideously painful. None of them constitutes an acceptable excuse for going ahead with a dud project; yet dud creative projects frequently go ahead, after they should have been stopped, for one, or another, or all three reasons.

With regard to the first two, it is the manager's responsibility to allow for contingencies within the original plans which were drawn up at the briefing stage. Managers all too frequently rely on creatives hitting the nail precisely on the head first time. It is reasonable to expect carpenters to strike nails home accurately, every time; it is unreasonable to expect creatives to produce brilliant ideas likewise. Creatives who fail repeatedly end up in dire straights. Until that point a degree of cautious indulgence is necessary, and delays must be built into the schedule.

The same is true of financial reserves. Ideally, the manager will provide for them, but not publicize the fact – as contingency funds have an unhappy propensity to evaporate, once their existence is known. No manager can, or ever should, attempt to insure against all manner of disastrous delays and bungles; but all managers should be ready to expect the unexpected. (On major projects, consideration should always be given to taking out professional insurance cover, if the premiums are not excessive.)

With regard to the third difficulty, it may be unpleasant, but the manager cannot afford to be fainthearted, as David Puttnam states:

'Creative work must be rejected quickly and cleanly. It's not something to dwell over.'

Michael Grade and Christopher Bland agree:

'There's only one way to handle rejection and that's to be absolutely blunt and honest and clean. You can't let people down lightly. You have to say, "Look I'm sorry, we're not going to do it for this reason or that reason". Rejection's got to be handled on the basis of straightforwardness and honesty.

'You just have to do it, and recognize that it is painful.'

Tim Bell, while not denying the necessity of handling rejections firmly, finds a tiny bit of dissembling helpful:

'You are not allowed to say, "I don't like it," as the basis for your rejection. That's one of the fundamental disciplines for anybody managing creatives. You can say whether you like something or not, though even that you have to be careful of, but you must certainly not make the fact that you don't like it the reason why it shouldn't go forward. Your rejection has to be on rational and logical and strategic grounds rather than emotional grounds.'

Paul Hamlyn and David Puttnam agree with Bell, that it is desirable to make the rejection sound objective rather than purely subjective. Michael Grade and Christopher Bland emphatically disagree. Here are Grade's views:

'I would never do that. I would give reasons. I would say, "I think it's too expensive for what the return is," or "The risks are too great," or "You haven't got this right," or "This is no good".

Then you have a dialogue. But at least you're arguing from the basis of honesty.'

Whichever way you handle it, and different managers obviously approach the problem in different ways, rejection must never be baulked. Only an idiotic manager, with no sense of priorities and no interest in long-term employment will allow poor work to be progressed because he is unable to overcome the difficulties involved in killing it.

Wally Olins has deliberately structured his systems to dissolve away many of the problems of amendment and rejection. He says:

'If you operate in a structure such as ours, where you have constant meetings, where you regularly see what is going on and you are absolutely honest with each other, then you won't get to a situation in which there is an internal presentation at which creative work is rejected . . . The physical layout of this building is such that people have to talk to each other all the time, and to show people their work.'

Olins even makes the same system succeed in his relationships with clients:

'Nothing will go forward that the client would not like because we go through the development process internally and we go through it externally, too. The client is constantly involved in the development of the idea. The manager's job is to persuade the client that the idea is right, and it may be necessary to spend months doing that.'

Olins' approach is initially very time-consuming, and initially, therefore, expensive. However, among the greatest costs all creative businesses bear are the costs of rejection. The costs of beginning again; of doing the same thing twice, three times or more; of bringing new creatives onto a project where others have failed; of sapped morale and dwindling confidence – all these, added together, will far outweigh the cost, as Olins believes, of doing things correctly (if expensively) in the first place.

It is obvious that not all creativity could be handled under Wally Olins' system. It is rarely, if ever, possible for photographers and journalists, or authors and composers, to be constantly supervised or to work in teams. Nor, as we've seen, is the system acceptable to all creatives; nor would the cost-per-project always justify such a level of management involvement. But his principles could be more widely applied, and with considerable success.

Finally, on the subject of amendment and rejection, the manager should always aim to minimize the pain inflicted by handling the situation as subtly and sensitively as possible. Here are five rules which will help make the distasteful marginally more palatable:

- Be at pains to be fair – point out the good elements in the work, as well as the bad; and make clear that you are sympathetic to the problems.

- Control your non-verbal communication – non-verbal communications often say more than the words we use, especially to perceptive creatives; this is especially true during criticisms and confrontations, when they are looking for tiny glimmers of reassurance and support. Remember Paul Hamlyn's cuddles.

- Don't rush – the creatives have probably spent a long time on their work, and it is of much importance to them; don't reject it after a second's glance, or indeed without a second glance.

- Seek areas of agreement – try hard to get the creatives to understand and agree to at least some of your criticisms, otherwise they are likely to harbour resentments which will later blossom like tropical plants in a hothouse.

- Summarize conclusions – such meetings are often emotional, so it is crucial to summarize at the end what has been agreed, and what is going to be done without bullying, but in order clarify any muddle; and it is usually a good idea to confirm the conclusions in writing soon afterwards.

When the unhappy meeting is over, Blanchard and Johnson offer the following advice in *The One Minute Manager*:[6] stand up, walk with the person to the door, and make a fleeting but encouraging physical contact – putting your arm quickly around the person's shoulders is best. It may sound irksome, but it works wonders on creatives who've just been battered about a bit.

Footnotes

■

1. Raudsepp, E. (1980) *Nurturing Managerial Creativity*: Dalton Communications Inc.
2. in Goldstein, M. L. (1985) *Op. cit.*
3. Storr, A. (1972) *Op. cit.*
4. Wordsworth, W. *I Wandered Lonely as a Cloud. . .*
5. Kirkwood, W. B. (1983) *Op. cit.*
6. Blanchard, K. and Johnson, S. (1983) *Op. cit.*

10

The Marketing of Creativity

■

With characteristic perversity the marketing of creativity is almost the exact antithesis of the marketing of all other goods and services. Indeed, purists might argue that the marketing of creativity is not really marketing at all.

The accepted textbook definition of marketing describes it as a process which begins with the consumer and tracks back to the manufacturer. First, consumers are asked what products they want; the manufacturer then develops products he believes will meet those wants; the manufacturer then tests the products on the consumers; only then, if and when the products are acceptable, does the manufacturer produce them and aim to persuade consumers to buy them. In the creative industries things happen the other way around. The 'manufacturer' decides what to produce, and then aims to persuade consumers to buy. Definitionally speaking, the creative industries are production-led rather than marketing-led, and they always will be.

However, the current textbook definition of marketing, which emanates from the packaged goods industries, is unnecessarily narrow. Unquestionably the best and most successful creative organizations pay close and continuous attention to what their customers want. They use their experience, intuition, flair, hunches and judgment. They use their eyes, ears and – though rarely in the olfactory sense – their noses. They study trends and fashions with far greater concentration than their peers in other industries. They have no choice, because for them change is perpetual and change is of the essence. However, they do not ask consumers what they want; nor – with one or two exceptions, which we shall note – do they test their products on consumers prior to production. In other words, they do little or no product research. To marketing people in other fields this would be anathema: the antithesis of true marketing.

The reasons why managers in the creative industries normally eschew 'product' research are two-fold: one economic, the other even more fundamental. The economic reason derives directly from our earlier cost-per-project analysis. The vast majority of creative projects are far too small to bear the cost, and the time, necessary for market research. Fashion garments, individual television and radio programmes, music, records and books (with one notable exception, to which we'll return) do not justify the investment, on a product-by-product basis. The more fundamental reason is that market research is a notoriously inaccurate means of assessing consumers' future tastes in creativity, for a multiplicity of reasons.

First, in many instances creative industries seek to lead and change tastes rather than follow them. To pre-test next year's fashions, or next year's musical sound, is impossible. The fashions, the sound, will not take off unless they are promoted with a great deal of press and television publicity (equals hype); unless they are accepted and adopted by opinion leaders; unless their mood and tone matches the moment. None of these crucial factors can be built-in to prior product research. If, to take a simple example, the Princess of Wales finds a particular garment fetching its sales are likely to boom forthwith. Unfortunately the Princess of Wales is unlikely to reveal her next year's apparel to market researchers.

Second, the great majority of individual creative products are bought by tiny minorities of the population. There are very, very few books, or records, or fashion garments, which sell in millions. Two million people is approximately five per cent of all UK adults. Market research techniques are not nearly exact enough to identify with any precision the tastes and requirements of so small a minority. (Every one per cent level of inaccuracy represents 20 per cent of the total five per cent.)

Third, for a majority of creative products (as was noted in Chapter 4) there is a chasm between concept and execution. The precise ways in which any idea or concept is executed will greatly effect its acceptability. Neither the plot of Hamlet, for example, nor a description of the Mona Lisa, makes either sound rivetting. So that while most other consumer products can be tested out in concept form, in advance of production, most creative products cannot. Consequently, creative products must usually be 'manufactured' before they can be tested – by which time many costs will already have been incurred, and many decisions irrevocably taken.

Fourth, for many, if not most, creative products the most powerful sales generator is word-of-mouth publicity. This is unarguably true in the movie, book, music and fashion industries. The companies involved seek as much publicity as they can, and sometimes bolster it with paid-for advertising. But these efforts merely kick-start the fly-wheel. Without the support of word-of-mouth publicity, the fly-wheel soon grinds to a halt. There is no market research technique which can simulate word-of-mouth publicity; and even if there were, there is no way of knowing in advance whether or not any particular creative product is going to generate it. (In the record industry, TV and radio plugs are the equivalent of word-of-mouth publicity – the mouth, in this case, being the disc jockey's.)

Fifth, whereas consumers in most product fields can describe with reasonable precision what they want a product to do, and criticize with reasonable clarity the failings of products they don't like, the problems of specification and analysis in the creative fields make this all but impossible. We have already seen that even experienced managers of creativity find it difficult to specify creative projects in advance. (It's the 'amorphous' problem once more.) In most creative industries, those who can respond to the products and describe their reactions become highly-paid critics: they are the fashion, music, cinema and architectural correspondents of newspapers and magazines. Ordinary members of the public, often lacking the necessary vocabulary, cannot begin to cope. To quote The Burton Group's Richard Birtchnell:[1]

'Ask the consumer directly to nominate designs, styles and colours and few will be able to tell you. The best you can hope for is, "I need something for a dinner party".'

To overcome, or rather outflank, all these difficulties, several creative industries have become extremely proficient at gauging consumer response to new products exceedingly rapidly, in the stores. The leading garment and record companies, for example, obtain immediate day-by-day computerized sales data, usually from a carefully chosen panel of retail outlets. Future sales can then be predicted with a fair degree of accuracy. Manufacturing orders can be instantly geared-up or geared-down, to be ready either to meet heavy demand or to minimize over-production. To quote Birtchnell again:

'To operate successfully in the fashion business you need to be clairvoyants on surfboards.

'What the surfer does is go out into the ocean feeling the waves, and when a good one comes along he paddles like hell to get onto it. Then rides it for all its worth before it goes crashing into the rocks.'

Nonetheless, and despite the formidable problems, some of the creative industries do engage in product pre-testing, when the cost-per-project makes it worthwhile, not to say imperative. The two industries which most use such market research are advertising and films. In neither are the techniques universally or unequivocally accepted; in neither have they eliminated the risk of failure – far from it; in both there are many case histories of occasions when tests have clearly miscarried; in both there are many case histories of projects on which they have clearly been of assistance.

In the film industry, new movies are occasionally pre-tested at concept stage when the script has been drafted and putative stars chosen, but before a final commitment to filming has been made. Such testing was more commonplace in the 1960s and 1970s than it is today. It has fallen out of fashion partly because of some famous occasions when it has gone spectacularly wrong. The concept of *Star Wars* is said to have done poorly in research, and as a result the film was rejected by two major film companies. Likewise, *ET* tested badly and as a result was turned down by Columbia, before being accepted by Universal and becoming the most successful motion picture of its time. In both cases, the gap between concept and execution was one with which the research could not cope. If the films had not been made as well as they were, they might indeed have failed. But then they *were* made as well as they were – emphasizing the vital influence that the quality of a creative product's execution has on its chances of success. And thus emphasizing the fallibility of such concept tests.

Almost every major movie, however, is nowadays screened after it has been filmed, but before it is launched publicly. In both the United States and Britain the research companies which specialize in these tests have amassed sufficient data to enable them to compare the test performance of each new movie with hundreds of predecessors. The sample audience is interrogated with questionnaires that have been honed, over the years, to provide clear and useable responses. As a result of such research, for example, the ending of *Fatal Attraction* was reshot three months after filming had been 'completed'. Most film production contracts now include a contingency allowance for the extra filming that may be necessary if the research so indicates.

Equally importantly, these test screenings identify which sectors of the population enjoy the film and which do not, and why they enjoy it or do not. Publicity, advertising and promotional material can then be aimed precisely at the appropriate target market, with the appropriate message. Managers in the movie industry now have considerable faith in the power of test screenings to identify the target market and to reveal why the film appeals to them.

No creative industry, however, is subject to as much research as advertising. Again this is a consequence of the high costs-per-project involved – though it must be understood that from the advertiser's point of view the cost-per-project is the total cost of the entire campaign: both the cost of producing the advertisements and the cost of the space or television time. Moreover, the commercial importance of getting the advertising right is increased beyond its own cost, because of the effects it can have on many other aspects of the advertiser's business: sales, manufacture, economies of scale and the rest. (The knock-on influence of packaging and other design work is similarly important, which is why designs and packaging are increasingly being similarly pre-tested.)

Innumerable weighty tomes have been written on the topic of advertising testing, and more and more appear each year. It must therefore suffice here to say that, as with films, advertisements can be tested both at initial concept stage and after they have been produced. The advantages and disadvantages are much the same for advertisements as for films. However, advertisements, unlike films, have no purpose in their own right, but are created in order to sell products. So the key factors which advertisement pre-tests aim to gauge are whether they are memorable and whether they are persuasive. It is comparatively easy, though quite expensive, to measure the former. It is impossible to measure the latter, so various surrogate assessments have been devised which deal with the question obliquely, but never provide an exact answer. Many major advertisers, particularly in the United States, have concentrated on measuring memorability, on the grounds that it can be done properly. In

Britain we have tended to concentrate on pre-tests which reveal whether or not advertisements communicate clearly and are likeable, on the grounds that if an advertisement meets those criteria it is logical to hypothesize that it will also be persuasive. It is impossible to validate this hypothesis, highlighting once again the difficulties inherent in the market research of creativity.

In addition to films and advertising, other creative industries which carry out a certain amount of market research into their products are packaging and design, as has already been mentioned, plus newspaper and magazine publishing. Many magazines have carried out research into the impact and sales effectiveness of their covers, and more recently book publishers have started to test jacket designs. (Magazine covers and book jackets can both be viewed as forms of packaging.)

Newspapers, and especially magazines, often produce and test 'dummies' of potential titles, in the style, shape and size of the proposed publication. Designs and packages are handmade, or printed in very small quantities for test purposes. Television companies, particularly in the United States, produce and test pilot films of potential new series and soaps – but Christopher Bland, for one, is sceptical of their value:

'One of the things the American networks desperately try to do is to take the unpredictability out of it. They try and write to formulae, they try to use research to replace – as opposed to supplement – the creative process. As a result, they produce a lot of diabolical work. It would be awfully nice if you could run a creative business like an iron foundry or a production line, but if you try the baby goes out of the bathwater. You can't do it.

'But people really do try. They say, "We've got the perfect formula . . . we've got this audience research which shows that all you need is two handsome guys and a good-looking girl and a train, let's make three of those" – and it doesn't work, yet they do it with situation comedies and drama all the time.'

In all creative testing, whatever the product or service, the closer the prototype is to the final product, the more reliable the results. Whenever the project is tried out in rough, conceptual form, the research findings must be interpreted with great caution.

Finally, on the subject of pre-testing creative work, it is worth noting the research methodology used by Readers' Digest Books, as it achieves exceptionally high levels of predictive accuracy. By normal book publishing standards, Readers' Digest books are blockbusters: the costs-per-project (and the anticipated sales) run into millions of pounds. So the Digest can afford to commit considerable financial resources to its pre-tests – which are done in stages, from initial name and concept through to the finally bound, printed and priced volume. At every stage the book is revised, and sharpened, in the light of the findings. Over the years, as in the film industry, the Digest has built-up a sizeable library of data, so that new projects can be compared, as they progress, with those that have gone before. And from the comparisons predictions can be made. Readers' Digest also pre-tests its compilation records – but while the contents of the compilation may be changed, the individual pieces of music themselves are not, and cannot be, amended.

The basic reason for the validity of the Readers' Digest's research system is not simply the meticulous care with which it is carried out, important though that is. The difference between the Digest and other publishers is that the Digest both sells its books and records by mail and carries out its research by mail. In other words, the research technique exactly replicates the sales method used, in terms both of creative content and target market. For the tests, the Digest draws upon a representative sample of those households which it finally intends to mail; and then sends them descriptive leaflets which approximate more and more closely to the sales literature which will finally be used. Any creative business which sells its products by post could employ the same techniques, and some mail-order clothes companies already do so, albeit on a lesser scale. But the great majority of creative organizations, which sell their wares in less controllable ways, are unable to take advantage of such tightly controllable testing techniques.

In any event, even the Digest willingly admits that the finest research techniques available are no substitute for editorial flair. The research can provide aims and directions, but the creatives must produce the goods. Similarly, the movie marketing people acknowledge that test screenings can uncover the faults in a film, but only the writer and director can correct them. From the creative manager's viewpoint, the attitudes of the creatives to market research will in large measure determine whether or not such research is worthwhile.

Most creatives' attitudes to market research are equivocal. On the one hand, they value, indeed are often thrilled by, the general public's opinions of their creativity. They enjoy the very notion of people looking at, concentrating upon and discussing their work. On the other hand, they firmly believe that the general public has neither the talent nor the sensitivity to criticize their work meaningfully. They subconsciously feel the public should respond to their work emotionally, without being required to analyze and dissect it. This is how Tim Bell describes advertising creatives:

'They're completely blind to the consumer. That's something they have in common with newspaper editors, and television men. All of them have this arrogance, that it is not necessary for them to know what the people they communicate with think. Or rather, they think they know already, without checking. They just don't feel it's necessary to check. When you do some research into an idea, or a piece of advertising, and the findings show people didn't understand it, the creatives reply, "They should have done".

'They're like football players, who want to be seen to be playing football better than each other, and they're less interested in the opinions of the crowd, or the opinions of the manager, than in the opinions of each other.'

In the advertising industry, where testing is held to be of great importance, a new breed of specialists has come into existence whose principal function is to act as an interface between market research and the creatives. These specialists, called account planners, are researchers who are particularly sympathetic to creativity. Their job is to test creative work among the general public (or the specific target market), and then to report the research findings to the creatives. Good account planners – and it is proving surprisingly difficult to find individuals able to fulfil the role – help the creatives to understand and accept research findings, even findings which are highly critical. (There is no problem in getting creatives to understand and accept research findings which are laudatory!) Some researchers in the movie industry have a similar role, though it has not there been identified as a specific and separate job function. In those other creative industries where the testing of creativity occasionally takes place, it is the manager's role to smooth the communications path between the creatives and research.

At last the creative product is right, or at least as right as the manager and the creatives know how to make it. It is time for it to be sold. At this point each of the creative industries goes its own way. Films are not sold in the same way as fashions, books are not sold in the same way as television programmes, buildings are not sold in the same way as greetings cards. Indeed, even within each industry different companies and organizations go about their marketing in completely disparate ways. Creativity is essentially a production function: creatives are employed to produce things, not to sell them.

Nonetheless, certain strands do appear to run through the marketing of many of the creative industries, as follows:

- Advertising is usually of little importance – advertising-to-sales ratios are minuscule in the books, records, fashion, design, television programme and even movie industries; and the creative industry which probably uses advertising to promote its goods least of all . . . is advertising itself.

- Sales in many creative industries are greatly influenced by journalists and critics, whose comments in both public and specialist media are highly influential – the manager should ensure that he knows as much as possible about the significant commentators in his field, and wherever possible get to know them personally.

- Publicity in the creative industries is frequently generated by the staging of events to which the journalists and critics feel impelled to come – premières, parties, fashion shows, stunts. People within each industry get bored and fed-up with such events, but they must never be neglected; on the contrary, as much effort as possible should go into making them bigger, better and more original than competitors'.

- Word-of-mouth publicity, as has already been noted, is always of great importance – and this can be stimulated, to some considerable degree, by the originality and impact of events and stunts; note the publicity which Richard Branson generates for Virgin.

- Opinion leaders, as has likewise been noted, are also exceedingly influential in most creative fields – this is partly because the public is uncertain of its creative tastes, partly because the activities of opinion leaders keep them, and the products they use, in the public eye. For the manager, the employment of opinion leaders offers considerable publicity potential; unlike the Princess of Wales, very few are impervious to sponsorship.

- Diversity is an essential element in the marketplace – it is inherent in the nature of creativity, as we've seen, that people seek variety. Singularly few creative products gain even one per cent market share, insofar as it is possible to define market shares. The manager must therefore always be working to offer his market as much variety as it needs, rather than aiming to dominate it with a small range of products. To quote Richard Birtchnell once more: 'The individual's aspiration is to appear unique, but we as fashion retailers are only profitable if we sell in bulk'. The paradox is common throughout the creative industries, and must be an essential component of any marketing strategy.

The above six points are characteristic of the creative industries, and to a great extent differentiate them from other consumer goods industries. Other consumer goods industries normally depend on advertising; critics and journalists hardly ever write about them (with the exception of cars); critics and journalists rarely attend product launches; opinion leaders are quite unimportant (who knows which detergents or toothpastes they use?); and in the majority of markets a few brands hold a dominant market share between them, which is what most marketing people aim for.

Finally, on the subject of marketing, managers should always keep in mind that creatives look to them to sell their work, and feel bitter if they fail. As Paul Hamlyn puts it, anecdotally:

'You're telephoned in the middle of the night: "Why isn't my book on sale at Paddington Station?" '

There are exceptions – as there have been in almost every aspect of creativity management – but by and large creatives do not like selling their own work. They don't think themselves to be much good at it, and they aren't. So the manager who they know can sell their work quickly wins their trust. Exaggerating the point a little, Tim Bell says:

'The real reason creative people have respect for you is that

you've got the guts to go and sell their work. And you can sell
it better than they would be able to.'

How a business goes about its marketing, marketing people are prone
to boast, will define the structure of the business. Without doubt the
ways in which creativity is marketed mould the structure of the
manager's role. In industries where the requirements of the customer
can be discovered and defined with some precision, the manager can
transmit those requirements in clear instructions to the producers of
the goods. Nobody would dream of arguing that the customer's
requirements should not be met. In the creative industries the customer's requirements can rarely be discovered, and never defined
with any precision. So the manager is always second-guessing. He is
second-guessing the customers when briefing the creatives, and
second-guessing them again when the creatives present their work
for acceptance. The manager permanently walks a tightrope, with
the uncertain demands of the marketplace on one side, the uncertain
output of creatives on the other. If either side becomes too turbulent
he will get blown off balance. To be a successful creative manager it
is essential to be adept at coping with customers, and colleagues, as
well as being adept at coping with creatives. It is essential, in other
words, to be a dab hand at marketing as well as at manufacturing.

Footnote

■

1. Birtchnell, R. (1989) *Op. cit.*

11

Fun and Profit

■

'If you're not in business for fun or profit, what the hell are you doing here?' quipped Robert Townsend in his iconoclastic management best-seller, *Up The Organisation*.[1] We'll return in a moment to whether or not the management of creativity is fun; indubitably it can be profitable. The top managers in advertising, newspaper and magazine publishing, television, sales promotion, movies, records and fashion all earn more than a handsome crust each year. Sir Ralph Halpern's annual £1,000,000 or so pay cheque is exceptional, but not that exceptional. Book publishing might be thought to be the Cinderella of the creative industries; but fortunes can be made even in book publishing, to which the many publishers on the list below bear witness.

Thirteen of those named in the *Sunday Times* 1989 chart of the 200 Richest People in Britain work in the creative industries – and that excludes Paul McCartney (joint 83rd in the chart with £80 million) and Elton John (158th with £40 million), both of whom are principally performers though they now do more than a little management on the side. Excluding some 70 members of the aristocracy on the list, the 13 represent ten per cent of the remaining 130. Admittedly, several of the 13 have made a proportion of their total wealth from other interests – property, retailing, investment and so on; and admittedly several of them inherited a fair proportion of their wealth – but that simply means their predecessors were successful in the management of creativity, too. On the other side of the balance sheet, a goodly number of individuals who have made tidy sums from the management of creativity were not on the list, or were listed as being in another kind of business because that is their principal source of income. Here then, in alphabetical order, are the lucky 13:

	£million		
Sir Bernard Ashley	166	42nd	Fashion & retailing
Richard Branson	125	Joint 51st	Music & business
Antony Crosthwaite-Eyre	77	86th	Publishing
Sir Terence Conran	56	109th	Design & retailing
Paul Hamlyn	164	43rd	Publishing
Michael Heseltine	60	Joint 100th	Publishing & property
Lewis Family	50	Joint 116th	Fashion
Mike Luckwell	30	Joint 188th	Television & publishing
Robert Maxwell	675	11th	Publishing
Viscount Rothermere	153	44th	Newspaper publishing
Saatchi Brothers	35	Joint 178th	Advertising
Earl of Stockton	100	Joint 64th	Publishing
Brian Thomson	100	Joint 64th	Publishing

Having got this far with *Creative People* you might be excused for thinking that they richly deserve every penny of their wealth, because managing creatives is so painful. Not so. They may well deserve every penny of their wealth because managing creatives is so difficult; or because the creative industries are so fiercely competitive and the ability to manage creatives is so rare; or because managing creatives is so taxing, so demanding, so exhausting; but not because it is painful. Not one of the managers of creativity who have contributed to this book find it anything but exciting, enjoyable and exhilarating. This may be because they are all exceptionally good at it, and people naturally tend to enjoy doing the things they are good at. Equally, they probably would not have dedicated their careers to the management of creativity had they found it a dreadful drudge. As was suggested in Chapter 5, those individuals who gain great pleasure from creativity gravitate towards the creative industries. Those who don't, don't. (Or if they inadvertently find themselves working in a creative industry they shift themselves out of it pretty damn quickly.)

Having said which, it is indisputable that the managers who work in creative industries enjoy gratifications unavailable in any other walks of life. As leading business writer William Davis puts it:[2]

'Innovation is surely the most exciting part of business life. It can also be one of the most frustrating. It can wreck careers as well as make them. But there is nothing to compare with the thrill of finding a new idea and turning it into reality.'

Creativity being a people business, it is hardly surprising that much of the thrill comes directly from working with creatives:

'I feel terribly lucky to be in this profession because the people I deal with, difficult as they are, and neurotic as they are, are interesting and fulfilling in lots of ways.' (Paul Hamlyn)

'Working with creatives is a very rewarding and stimulating experience, they tend to look at things from a lateral viewpoint which can be very refreshing.' (Sir Ralph Halpern)

'Sometimes you take a gamble with somebody – "I like the way he talked about a programme, I think this person has got a bit of creative flair" – and you put them in the job. Then you watch them blossom and they come through with some marvellous ideas. Watching them grow, and get confidence, and maturity of judgment – that's a great feeling.' (Michael Grade)

'Their generation of ideas is fantastically stimulating. With the very best creative people they introduce you to a way of looking at something which is totally different to the way you yourself look at it, so they open your horizons. The really great creative people are marvellous to work with.' (Tim Bell)

But if people are the source of most of the joys, they are also the source of quite a few woes:

'Pretentiousness and preciousness drive me mad. Creative people who feel that in some way, shape or form they do not necessarily have to subscribe to normal rules of human behaviour – that's the thing I cannot tolerate. Someone who is driving from A to B on location and insists he doesn't share a car, because his contract says he gets sole use of the car – it's a misuse of resources, a misuse of power, a misunderstanding of the entire process. It's destructive.

'The *great* talents don't have those pretentious qualities. Those pretentious qualities are armour, which moderately

talented people surround themselves with, to hide their insecurities.' (David Puttnam)

'The most irritating aspects of working with creative people are
their arrogance, their egotism and their total self-centredness,
their feeling that the world has to revolve around them, that
time doesn't exist, that time is their property: their complete
selfishness in relation to other human beings. That is the worst
conceivable aspect of working with creative people, that they
are babyish and selfish. They are not all like that, only a small
minority are like that, and if anybody behaves to them as they
behave to other people they are bitterly resentful.

'If they are young and immature emotionally, which they
frequently are, and if they become successful very quickly, the
pitiful remnants of any self-discipline that may have been drilled
into them at school or at home disappear totally and they become
completely unmanageable.' (Wally Olins)

Wally Olins' word picture of some of the less attractive aspects of
the creative personality mirrors the portrait delineated in Chapter 3.
And the fact that creatives need to be endlessly reassured, flattered,
massaged and cuddled has already been discussed at length. In the
end, happily, the ecstasies greatly outweigh the agonies. The
bewitching enchantment of enabling creatives to create obliterates
the petty irritations and irksomeness of coping with their personality
problems. Here then, are the self-defined job satisfactions of people
in love with their work:

'Whenever I've felt that the logistics of a job were getting me
down – not another set of board minutes to approve, or another
executive committee meeting to attend, or not another boring
pile of correspondence to deal with – whenever I feel anything
like that, I just talk to a designer or a director and they will
convey by the enthusiasm of their response the excitement that
they feel about the particular project they are working on. You
suddenly feel the whole thing is worthwhile because the pleasure you are getting from your job is precisely that of enabling
them to do what it is that they can do well; you feel you are
almost giving birth to something, or rather acting as a sort
of midwife, making a good thing possible that wouldn't have

happened unless you had given the go-ahead. That is a huge reward and lifts one's job out of the ordinary. So the rewards of managing creativity are far greater than the strains and pressures. "Enabling" is the word which describes it best.' (Jeremy Isaacs)

'This amazing and unpredictable process sometimes results in work of which you are really proud, really glad to be associated with, really glad to see your company's name on. That's a terrific feeling, even if you only had an indirect involvement. It's like having a baby. My role, corporately, is that of the grandfather. I have a limited involvement, and far less of the pain. But even by association I take considerable pride, as the grandfather of the child. That's the greatest pleasure.' (Christopher Bland)

'The pleasure for me is being part of a harmonious team who love working with each other and share a common dream. You see I actually love watching a great talent performing as *part* of a team. That's a great art, and great artists can do it – sublimate themselves to the work in progress . . . It is being part of something which is bigger than any individual, no matter how gifted. When you're working on a film that has something to say, everyone is swept along, it carries them, and you know you are part of something special.' (David Puttnam)

'I adore it. This is a great gambling business, and I love it. It is full of surprises, daily. A publisher could not operate if he didn't like the excitement of a punt, even if he were in academic or educational publishing. One looks at something, one says this is right, one goes for it – and often you fall flat on your face. But when it works it's great.' (Paul Hamlyn)

'It's marvellous to produce things that have made an impact on civilization. It may only be a very small impact, it may only be a footnote, but it is an impact in social, cultural and economic terms. To take part in the development of the community as we are doing in a lot of our work, visually and culturally, is marvellous. I can't conceive of anything I would rather do.' (Wally Olins)

But in all the thrills and spills, ups and downs, highs and lows of the creative manager's life, he must never forget the simple kernel of his *raison d'être*, which David Puttnam describes admirably:

'One last thing. An original idea, a great idea, is God-given. And an original idea is fragile, it can very, very easily get trampled on. The manager's job, first and foremost, is to protect the integrity of that original idea.'

It's profitable, it's fun, and it's worthwhile. What more can you ask of a job?

Footnotes

■

1. Townsend, R. (1970) *Up The Organization*, London: Michael Joseph.
2. Davis, W. (1989) 'They All Laughed', *Global Business Magazine*, April.

Index

∎